What they're saying about

"The wisdom and knowledge contained in G... wish I'd had it when I was starting out as an entertainer! It's a marvellous achievement and could be your secret weapon."
- Michael Feinstein

"Gary Williams' book is a godsend for singers. It's not only a bible for aspiring performers, but also helps pros focus in ways they might not have previously considered. It's a must-read whether you sing jazz, pop, rock, opera or cabaret. His secrets are worth their weight in gold!"
- Harold Sanditen, Open Mic host

"A beautifully conceived and crafted tutorial. Hugely instructive, hugely accessible and hugely revealing (i.e. 'the secret of things that come in three's')."
- Jeff Harnar, performer/director

"What a great book! Well written, full of humour, knowledge and information."
- Joan Jaffe, 2012 M.A.C Award winner

"This is the best guide ever written for the aspiring cabaret singer. Gary Williams' generous sharing of his own secrets provides so much valuable information that it deserves to be read by anyone wanting a career in cabaret."
- Ruth Leon, Artistic Director

""[Cabaret Secrets] opens up three choices for prospective Cabaret performers: (1) They can do a Performing Arts course at University and get an ongoing £20,000 student loan debt for life... or (2) They can take their chances on Britain's Got Talent with odds of about 500,000 to 1 , or (3) They can buy Gary's book for £14.50 and do what it says."
- Gordon Sapsed

GARY WILLIAMS

CABARET SECRETS

How to create your own show,
travel the world and get paid
to do what you love.

Published by Gary Williams, 172 Haverstock Hill, London NW3 2AT United Kingdom
www.cabaretsecrets.com

Cabaret Secrets
Copyright 2013 by Gary Williams
ISBN: 978-0-9576104-2-2

All rights reserved. No part of this book may be reproduced in any form or by any electronic or mechanical means including information storage and retrieval systems, without permission in writing from the author. The only exception is by a reviewer, who may quote short excerpts in a review.

License Statement
This book is sold subject to the condition that it shall not, by way of trade or otherwise, be lent, re-sold, hired out or otherwise circulated in any form of binding or cover other than that in which it is published and without a similar condition including this condition being imposed on the subsequent purchaser.

Contents

Preface 1
Introduction 6
The Secrets
    Secret 1: Be Prepared 11
    Secret 2: It's All About You 19
    Secret 3: Be Sincere 28
    Secret 4: Use A Template 32
    Secret 5: How To Chat To An Audience
        (and not sound like a fake) 48
    Secret 6: Live Performance Can Seriously Damage
        Your Health (and Ego) 67
    Secret 7: Love Your Musicians 71
    Secret 8: Make It Look Good And It Will
        Sound Twice As Good 84
    Secret 9: Record a CD 102
    Secret 10: Listen To Advice, But Be Careful How You Give It 108
    Secret 11: Talent Is Only The Starting Point 112
    Secret 12: Find Your Audience 122
    Secret 13: Rock Stars Live Like Nuns 138
    Secret 14: How To Get An Agent 154
    Secret 15: The Best Piece of Travel Advice, Ever 167
    Secret 16: Simon Cowell Is Not Your Friend 173
Conclusion 180
Glossary 193
Appendix: Show Analyses 209
Acknowledgements 226
About The Author 228

Preface

It's been around for over 100 years, is difficult to define, and just when you think it's gone away forever, there's another comeback. No, not The Rolling Stones, I'm talking about the subtle art of cabaret.

Give me a few hours and I'll show you how to produce your own show, travel the world and get paid to do what you love.

Andrea Marcovicci, one of its greatest exponents, describes cabaret like this:

> ...an evening of song and stories in an intimate space that shatters the 'fourth wall'. Part stand-up comic, part balladeer, part evangelist; today's performer often has a theme that unifies the evening, knows a great deal about the music they're singing, and shares that information in witty and inventive ways. At its best, cabaret can amuse, entertain, and inform... it can dazzle you, catch you unawares and make you weep. The audience participates in a direct, emotional conversation with the artiste...

Never quite the mainstream and often the target of moral crusaders, cabaret clubs have taken many forms since their beginnings in the late 19th-century. From Parisian hangouts for poets and the seedy burlesque rooms of Berlin, to America's mob-run speakeasies and later stylish supper clubs, cabaret has always been about intimacy and audience interaction.

Cabaret is enjoying a resurgence. Jaded by overly produced pop groups, and super-slick TV performances, people want the raw unpredictably of a live show.

These days an evening of cabaret could mean a cross-dressing bassoonist, a jazz ensemble, a snake charmer, an octogenarian poet, a crooner in a tuxedo or a burlesque dancer with a hula-hoop.

Each cabaret discipline has its own nuances and since I've never charmed a snake or played the bassoon, this book is aimed at singers. The type of music you sing is irrelevant. We'll be learning from Amy Winehouse and Take That, as well Michael Feinstein and Steve Ross. The size of the room doesn't matter. With the right skills any singer can make a theatre or concert hall feel as intimate as the smallest cabaret room. What counts - the defining factor of any cabaret performance as far as I'm concerned - is making a personal connection with the audience. Whether it's Celine Dion in Las Vegas, Tara Khaler on a cruise ship or Jeff Harner in a New York club, it's that connection - the ability to create a dialogue with the audience and share something of yourself - that we'll be exploring here.

Frank Sinatra liked to describe himself as a saloon singer, even though he'd sing to thousands at a time. He had the ability to make everyone feel as though he was singing just to them, even in a huge stadium.

Lisa Martland, critic for The Stage and editor of Musical Theatre Review told me:

> Some of the best-known cabaret performers - the likes of Barbara Cook, Elaine Stritch and Liza Minnelli -

rarely play the small rooms nowadays, so the intimacy of a performance is lost. However, there are still occasions, when they're appearing in theatres or even arenas, that their delicate touch with a certain composition can still touch the heart. In fact, just one performance of a song can stay with you forever.

According to critic Mark Shenton:

> Barbara Cook remains the gold standard of cabaret performance, because she has it all; and because of that, she can achieve the cabaret ideal, which is to make the audience member feel like they are being personally addressed by her, whatever the size of the room. She's made me feel that in Carnegie Hall, the Metropolitan Opera House, the London Coliseum and Feinstein's in New York, a comparatively tiny room.

Performer and founder of the London Cabaret Awards, Paul L. Martin believes the current resurgence in cabaret has a lot to do with our busy lifestyles and attention spans. He told me:

> Cabaret offers the opportunity to socialise and enjoy a show where you can interact with the performers. It seems, for many, this is preferable to sitting quietly in a dark theatre for two hours and applauding at the 'appropriate' moments. Using traditional theatre as a juxtaposition, you can often see the very same performers from a West End show in a more intimate, and often unique cabaret setting for a fraction of the price. Not to be sniffed at in these difficult economic times. Above all though I believe it's the immediacy

and the spontaneity of cabaret that's so exciting for audiences and performers alike; stripping away the fourth wall and dealing with whatever happens in the room is something you cannot rehearse.

The challenge

Despite its resurgence, it's tough to make a living solely as a cabaret artiste in traditional clubs. It's hard to find an audience and many venues have simply disappeared. Andrea Marcovicci told me, "With determination it is possible to make a living in cabaret rooms but since the downturn in the economy, one has to be realistic about fees."

Lisa Martland knows better than most the challenges any new cabaret artiste will face, "Cabaret is not an easy genre to break into or make any kind of living from. Artistes need to be prepared to put a huge amount of time and resources (if they are available) into self-promotion and marketing."

That's certainly the case for artistes offering lesser known fare to small discerning audiences but the good news is that mainstream cabaret isn't dead, it's just moved... to sea. The cruise ship industry is huge and getting bigger all the time. There you'll find intimate lounges, state-of-the-art theatres and a ready-made audience. For the right artistes, there's a lot of work out there and a good living to be made.

What you'll find here

I can't teach you how to sing. I've only just started having lessons myself, so when anyone asks me about head voices, semi-breves and rallentandos, I don't have a clue what they're talking about. I thought a diaphragm was a type of contraception.

When people ask for my advice on producing their own show I'm a little more confident. In fact, it's probably the only thing I know anything about.

When I told some of my peers I was planning on publishing all my 'secrets', they thought I was mad. "Information," they told me, "is your livelihood". Some of my peers felt that they had spent years learning how to produce shows, develop stage craft and ultimately, find great work - so why should I make it easy for everyone else to do the same?

Well, I don't buy that. Wherever you find success there'll always be somebody younger, more talented and better looking biting at your heels. You can either live in endless fear that they'll put you out of a job or relax and be confident in your own abilities.

Fortunately there are lots of great performers, promoters, managers, technicians and writers who've been happy to share their secrets in this book. I am sincerely grateful to them. Many have recorded audio interviews that you can listen to in full at cabaretsecrets.com or on the YouTube channel, www.youtube.com/c/cabaret secrets

Cabaret Secrets is a handbook packed with practical advice and insider knowledge. Though much of the advice applies to any kind of act in any kind of venue, I've written mainly with cruise ship singers in mind. Follow this guide and soon you'll be travelling the world and getting the applause (and the money) you deserve.

Remember to send me a postcard!

Gary Williams

Introduction

"Good afternoon Mr Williams. I am the Prince of Wales' Private Secretary. I understand you are looking for somewhere to warm up your voice."

"Oh, yes," I smiled, "do you have somewhere in mind?"

"This way please, Sir."

We took a short walk to a pair of exquisitely ornate doors, which he opened theatrically and announced, "The Music Room. Signor Pavarotti entertained her Majesty here last week. Will it do?"

I didn't answer straight away. My mind flitted back to my first singing engagement twelve years before. It was in a pub in Scunthorpe, the north of England. I had to get changed in the staff toilet.

"This will be fine," I told him.

Standing there on the plush red carpet of Buckingham Palace reminded me of how much had happened since that night up north. Back then all I dreamt about was being a professional entertainer singing the Great American Songbook. With this in mind I got some backing tracks, told everyone I had "an act" and waited for the phone to ring.

It did ring but it wasn't Capital Records. Two friends had broken down on the motorway and needed help. Fortunately they didn't want break down assistance, they wanted me to perform in their place that night. They offered me £50 and I accepted on the spot.

I threw everything in the car and sped off to Scunthorpe (the rough part). On the way I called my mum and asked her if she wanted to come and lend some moral support.

"Oh yes, I've heard of that pub..." she hesitated, "I'm not really sure it's quite the place for respectable people. Good luck, dear."

Forty minutes later I was inside a noisy bar heavy with cigarette smoke and packed with impatient inebriates braying for the promised entertainment. My mother was right. The only thing that would have bothered her more than the sticky carpet were all the tattoos. Somehow, in her mind, the tattoo represents everything that's wrong in the world. This includes anyone who drinks strong cider, wears an ankle bracelet or owns a deep fat fryer.

The landlord looked me up and down, his eyes lingering on my brand new sports jacket. "I wouldn't wear that in here if I were you."

The show began. I had expected a warm welcome, a few cheers perhaps, at least polite applause. What I got was general disinterest and a few blank stares. My heart sank. Obviously I'd interrupted their evening of drinking.

I persevered, but was clearly dying. I couldn't wait to get off the stage and I decided to finish with a medley of Cole Porter favourites. Half way through, the end in sight, a middle-aged woman with both an ankle bracelet and a tattoo (and probably a deep fat fryer at home) joined me on stage. Pint in one hand, cigarette in the other, she gyrated in front of me, blowing smoke in my face and pressing her fleshy thighs against mine. I was mortified. The audience went wild.

I was done. I took a quick bow and had almost left the stage when the chanting started. My dance partner had grabbed their attention, and now they all wanted more. "UB40, UB40..." Soon the whole audience were banging on the tables, shouting "UB40, UB40." I didn't know what to do. I have some vague recollection of UB40 in the 80s, but beyond that I was lost. As the chants grew louder I began to panic. What could I give them? Then it hit me. 'New York, New York'. There could hardly be a more perfect song for a crowd like this. It appeals to all ages and is loved by everyone, especially drunks.

"I don't have any UB40," I said, "but I do have this!" The famous introduction boomed from my speakers. I closed my eyes, said a silent prayer and sang for my life. I couldn't tell if they were cheering or booing. Probably both. It didn't matter. Three more minutes and I'd be safely in my car driving home. Opening my eyes for a peek at the crowd I spotted a large lady teetering on a barstool. She was leaning towards me, red faced and shouting,

"W-A-N-K-E-R! YOU W-A-N-K-E-R!"

I have never seen a look of such intensity on a face. I ploughed ahead, "I'll make a brand new start of it…" as she threw in a few hand gestures to make sure I hadn't missed the point.

When I'd finished, the room was in chaos. A small fight had broken out, a chair had been thrown, the dancing woman was on a table, and a small section of the crowd had begun singing UB40's 'Red, Red Wine'. The landlord surveyed the carnage, took the microphone from me, and said, "Until tonight I'd never heard of this lad. He's come here to our pub and I'll tell you what… he'll be coming back!"

I had my own thoughts on that matter, but for the time being I had to pack my gear away and get to my car without being accosted.

That was to be the first of many gigs in north England's pubs and clubs. They were tough but provided an invaluable training ground.

Help is at hand

You're reading this because you need help. Good help is hard to find. There are no cabaret schools, few cabaret consultants and hardly any of the numerous musical theatre schools offer any comprehensive training in the art of cabaret. And yet, it's the way thousands of singers make their living.

Good live entertainment in Working Men's Clubs has almost disappeared, which is cause for concern. It's where I and generations of performers learned their craft and served their apprenticeships. Having survived some of the clubs I worked, everything else seems a breeze. As Frank Sinatra said, "If you can make it there, you'll make it anywhere."

Artistic Director for Belinda King Productions, Lisa Cottrell, knows first hand the challenges a solo artiste can face:

> I hear a lot of singers say they want to go solo with their own cabaret. They often have no idea of how difficult it is - getting music arranged, finding the right agent and building up a reputation within the business are just a few of the hurdles they face. There are no sets, costumes or dancers to support you - you're on your own.

> Getting experience as a solo singer is vital and there are not many venues left where new performers can hone their craft. The demise of variety and the growth of television talent shows have created a breed of young performers who think that success comes instantly. It takes a lot of hard work, self-belief and determination to be a successful cabaret artiste.

> None of the audience care that you may have spent twelve hours waiting for your delayed flight, or that your luggage was lost in Istanbul and you're wearing a borrowed suit. You have to enjoy airports, packing, unpacking, meeting new people, the waiting around

and ultimately be happy with your own company, as I'm sure at times it's quite a lonely life.

She's right. Opportunities for aspiring cabaret artistes to polish their skills are few and far between. Who teaches these people how to structure a show? How to talk to an audience? How to get an agent?

For years after my inauspicious start in that English pub, I was desperate for someone to help me with my act. Old pros told me about "Act Doctors" who could be hired to observe an act and offer improvements. Apparently though there were none left. They'd all died along with variety. I was left to fend for myself, rely on my intuition and learn from my mistakes.

Of course, these days my shows change significantly from one venue to another. What's perfect for a small London jazz club might be hopeless on a large American cruise ship. Factors like audience demographic, nationality, age and the size of the room all have an impact on the show. I work to a set of self-imposed rules, which dictate my approach and help me customise every performance. It is those rules that I will share with you here in Cabaret Secrets.

I'm not going to teach you how to sing, improve your posture or how to arabesque. What I will do is show you how to create and present your own show. In these pages I'll share everything with you that I've learned so far, but before we get too carried away, let's see if you've really got what it takes.

The Secrets
Secret 1: Be Prepared

No one seems to know what it is or where it comes from. Apparently you either have it or you don't and Simon Cowell's made millions spotting it.

The 'X' factor. What is it? Why do you need it, and how can you get more of it?

Mark Shenton thinks there are some things you just can't buy:

> Great cabaret isn't just about the voice (though for me it has to start with it) and selecting great material to showcase it, but about the rapport and intimacy that the artiste establishes with the audience. Part of that is personality - which you can't buy, still less manufacture - but it's also about sincerity and passion.

Artistic Director of the London Olympics, Kim Gavin, has worked with some of the biggest names in the business and thinks the 'X' Factor is very difficult to define. He told me:

> The question is, do you want to watch them again?

That's the only way I could ever define it. So, do you want to watch Take That again? Yes, you do. Do you want to watch Boyzone again? No. The 'X' Factor is about much more than the music. It's an atmosphere or a persona on stage. Even though Leona Lewis has one of the most amazing voices, she doesn't relate to the audience. Yes, she sings brilliantly, but unless we get to know her and like her, it's not enough. There has to be something that makes you interested to see her again.

The 'X' seems to mean different things to different people. For me, 'X' equals charisma.

My dictionary defines charisma as "Personal attractiveness or interestingness that allows you to influence others." As performers it's our job to influence the moods of hundreds or thousands of 'others' every time we walk on stage.

There are lots of talented people out there. They might know jaw-dropping illusions, juggle six balls with ease or sing like angels, but a performer without charisma is like a canvas without paint.

So how can you get more of it?

Your natural personality counts for a lot. You have to love to share and communicate. In other words, you need to be a bit of a show-off. For many people, including me, Bobby Short will always be one of the very best cabaret performers – a unique voice, great pianist, witty, and he knows how to pick a song. He explained his draw to the stage like this, "I wanted to perform for the same reason most people do – attention. I do have some talent, but really, I wanted attention. We all want to be noticed in some way, and so you perform, you're noticed and you're constantly loved."

Lennie Watts is an 8 time MAC, 5 time Backstage Bistro, and 3 time Nightlife Award winner. He's been active in the New York cabaret scene for over 20 years and the only person to receive awards as an outstanding vocalist, director, producer, and booking manager. I think it's safe to say he knows what he's talking about. Here are his thoughts on what it takes to make it in cabaret:

> Anyone with life experience, a point of view, and the ability to tell a story can learn the art of cabaret. All of the other skills can be easily taught. The person attempting cabaret just needs to be open and willing to put themselves in an incredibly vulnerable, yet truly satisfying position.

In response to the much vaunted "You either have it or you don't" opinion, another MAC Award winner, Joan Jaffe says, "True, but if you only have it a little bit, with the proper guidance from the right people, there is hope."

Conductor, arranger and musician John Wilson thinks it's more than that though:

> I've learned that the greatest artists have music inside them; that no amount of training or education can give an artiste that certain star quality, that special something that will move an audience and communicate something directly to them.

Even if you're not brimming with that "certain star quality", I do believe charisma can be developed. Stage presence comes in part from confidence and there's no greater aid to confidence than experience. Marta Sanders, a New York cabaret artiste with over forty years in the business, told me, "The audience doesn't want to worry about you. You must be in control so they can relax. Don't show fear. Whatever happens, keep smiling." The more you perform, the more confident you'll become which allows your personality to shine through. Your performances will become more honest and sincere.

Whether they paint, walk the high wire, or sing - honesty and sincerity are the cornerstones of all great artistes. People recognise it, respond to it and love them for it. If you find large groups of people terrifying, now might be a good time to take the nearest available exit and consider a different career path.

Building confidence

LBC Talk Radio host, Anthony Davis, reckons there are three stages to building real confidence. First, there's that fearless, youthful confidence of the early 20s. These young people have only been told how wonderful they are and nothing's ever happened to suggest otherwise. Next, as they see a little more of the world, suffer a few knocks and gain a little wisdom, they realise they might not know everything after all. Their confidence takes a dip, they become more questioning and less impetuous. Then begins the long, slow recovery to a new kind of confidence founded in experience, truth and knowledge. This is the foundation of every truly self-assured performer. You carry around a new inner confidence, and because you know you know what you're doing, you don't have to work so hard. Just standing still on stage, projecting your energy can be enough to own the room.

It took me twenty years of performing to get there. Luckily you don't have to wait that long. Principal singer with the Ronnie Scott's Jazz Orchestra, Iain Mackenzie, has two words of advice for anyone who wants a shortcut: "Be prepared". Lisa Cottrell agrees. Her advice, "Be versatile, don't take anything personally, and most importantly - be prepared."

Be prepared

So it seems the way to find more of the elusive 'X' Factor is through preparation. John Wilson told me the only thing worse than an arrogant singer is an unprepared singer. "There are those," he says, "who simply don't realise just how good you have to be to stand before an orchestra and an audience. I like to work with singers who are completely prepared, who rehearse efficiently and then go up umpteen notches in the show."

> *"Before anything else, preparation is the key to success"*
> *Alexander Graham Bell*

There's no substitute for painstaking preparation and really knowing your stuff. Prepare your voice by warming up properly, know what you're going to say and when you intend to say it, make sure you've organised your music properly and everything is clear for the musicians, that you know your material backwards, your clothes are pressed and you understand your audience. The only reason I'm not terrified when I walk out on stage, is because I do everything possible to prepare myself. When the pressure's on, I know exactly what I'm doing.

Even for a show I've performed many times, I spend hours getting ready, going over every detail. I stand on the stage and walk through every song to decide how I'll use the space, when I'll use the microphone stand, what the lights will be doing, when I'll interact with the musicians and so on. I love spontaneity and surprises in my show but I'm always working from a secure foundation. Being on top of all the elements I can control means I'm free to worry about those I cannot. Will the band play well? Will my microphone work? How will the audience react?

I learned early on what can happen if you don't prepare.

When I started out, I'd open my show with Frank Sinatra and close with Roy Orbison. I needed a quick way to change from a tuxedo to a black shirt, so asked my mother for help. She found a tuxedo jacket in Oxfam, sewed a shirt-front and bow tie inside, split open the back and added two velcro strips to join it back together. I had exactly 6 seconds in the blackout between My Way and Pretty Woman to make the change. All I had to do was rip the velcro apart and remove the jacket before the lights came back on. I'd have a new look and the audience would be suitably astonished. That night, as My Way finished, the lights went out. 6... 5... I leaned forward to split the velcro apart. It didn't budge. 4... 3... The velcro was simply too strong. 2... 1... I panicked. Like Houdini in a water tank, I was on my knees, thrashing around, trying to escape from the jacket as though my life depended on it. And still nothing. I heard the unmistakable opening bars of Pretty Woman and the lights came up. Instead of a miraculous transformation from crooner to pop icon, the audience found me sitting on the floor, staring at them from the back of the stage, sweating and panic stricken. I was caught in the spotlight like an asylum escapee. After that, I made a promise to myself: rehearse everything.

Over the years I've had lots of things go wrong on stage. Scenery's fallen on my head, I've forgotten lyrics and I've turned up in the wrong town. Thankfully I've survived (relatively) unharmed. The more experience you have, the more you learn to cope with anything that's thrown at you, literally in some cases, and as your command of the stage grows, so does your confidence.

A little charm goes a long way
If you charm an audience and they really like you, there isn't much they won't forgive. As long as you're not phased when you miss a cue or introduce the wrong song, they'll be behind

you. In fact they'll like you even more for being real.

There are some pretty awful singers out there who wouldn't last five minutes in a recording studio, but put them in front of a live audience where their charisma shines through, and they can do no wrong. I'll never forget seeing one truly remarkable act. Unaware of his considerable vocal limitations he opened with the ambitious 'This Is The Moment', a song well out of his range, and gave us forty-five minutes of 'belters', each with limited success. It was enough to make his own mother wince. As he closed with 'The Music of the Night', complete with mask and a polyester cape, I sank in my chair out of shame for the poor man. The audience, however, had taken him to their hearts. As soon as he'd hit the last note they jumped to their feet, giving him a full standing ovation. I can still picture it now. The fella next to me cried, "This guy's incredible. Amazing!" I was astonished and, in truth, fascinated. I spent days trying to figure out how he did it (I wanted some of that). Then I realised - charisma. Sure, he sang their favourite songs, but crucially, he was sincere, he was likeable and he was genuine. They didn't care that he was flat, forgot his lyrics and his neck went red at the end of every song. They just liked him.

It works both ways

Audiences are not always so generous. It's fascinating (and terrifying) to see how quickly they can turn on a performer. I once saw a comedian, on the old QE2, tell a crass joke that offended a large part of his audience. He knew instantly he'd made a mistake, but it was too late. His next routine landed flat. Hardly anyone laughed. A few people got up to leave. More followed. Soon there was a steady stream of people heading for the exit. The comic panicked. He lost his place. Beads of sweat began to appear. No one was applauding and people actually took their seats again just to watch the poor man suffer. It was an agonising lesson in how quickly the veneer of confidence can disappear. Anyone can make a mistake, but had he prepared properly and taken better notice of his audience, he might have avoided this untimely public death.

Painstaking preparation means more confidence and confidence is the corner stone of charisma. If you're not quite there yet, fake it till you make it. Having actual talent helps, but as Kander and Ebb said, "Give them the old razzle dazzle and you'll get away with murder."

Ready? Let's get to work.

Secret 2: It's All About

Musical theatre performers are trained to ignore the audience. They immerse themselves in another character and as we look on, they pretend they're alone. We are voyeurs of their 'public solitude'. Cabaret is more personal than that. It's all about you.

Theme your show
Your show needs a strong theme, a 'hook' to draw the audience in and give it some structure. Chances are there's one particular genre of music that will form the foundation of your show: musical theatre, pop, rock and roll, swing etc. but ultimately your show should be about you.

People want to know why you perform, the highs and lows of your career, what inspires you. Rather than talking about your songs in general terms, talk about what they mean to you personally. If you trust the audience and give something of yourself, they will do the same for you. So whatever style of music you like to sing, remember you are the thread that holds it all together.

"Cabaret is a wonderful form of self-expression. Ask yourself, 'what do I need to say,' and then find songs and stories that tell that story." Liz Callaway

Jeff Harnar created a show called 'The 1959 Broadway Songbook', a theme that draws from anything you might have heard on Broadway that year. It allowed him to include songs from a whole range of musicals and even a rock-and-roll hit from the radio of a passing Chevy. It's a great hook. It gives the audience a good idea of what to expect while still allowing Jeff plenty of good material to draw on, and, as he told me, there are benefits beyond the repertoire:

> Theme shows have served me very well. I've found that audiences, venues, the press and booking agents like a strong 'hook' and a memorable title. They can inspire more promotional opportunities than my name alone ever could. By piggy-backing my name on to an established 'brand' like a songwriter, an era, Broadway, Hollywood and so on, I can attract a new audience. Even if they don't yet know who I am, their love of the brand will introduce my work to them.

Cruise Director João Wolf says:

> It's your responsibility as an entertainer to keep the audience's attention at all times. Your show should have a shape, a beginning, middle and end - like a movie. When you get this right, the audience is engaged and they forget about everything else; they follow you on your journey. If you're just singing a collection of songs without thinking about the dynamics of the show as a whole, you'll lose them.

I'm a crooner. I sing easy-listening, jazz and Latin music. When guests on a cruise ship in the middle of the Atlantic see 'Star of the West End's 'Rat Pack' Gary Williams sings the Great American Songbook', they know exactly what to expect. If they like that style, they'll come, if not, they'll go to the casino.

Themes like 'Broadway Divas' or 'Motown Million Sellers' are the 'hooks' that draw the audience in. This is why tribute acts are so popular, people know what they're going to get. 'Gary Williams pays tribute to Matt Monro' is a much stronger sell than just 'Gary Williams in Cabaret'. Of course, once you set audience expectations, you'd better make sure you come up with the goods and don't disappoint.

Deciding on a theme helps to define you and makes it easier to choose which songs you're going to sing.

Remember your audience

Don't make the mistake of forgetting who you're performing to. Check the demographic. If your audience is enjoying a gentle retirement you might want to cut your Madonna medley. If half of them are German and speak little English don't be surprised if no one laughs at your jokes. I recently discovered (by alarmingly light applause) that Neil Diamond never made it in Brazil. I also found, by accident, that everyone there knows and loves Nat 'King' Cole's 'When I Fall In Love'.

"Always treat your audience as partners not customers." James Stewart

Liz Callaway told me:

> Out of town, the audiences prefer to hear what they know, so I sing mostly recognisable songs (though I may try a new spin on them). In New York, or any city with an 'in the know' audience, I'll mix in lesser-known songs.

That's the smart approach. Singing fifty minutes of little known material may be a treat for those in the know, but if it's not right for your audience you will lose them, and probably your job. If you want to sing songs from the latest off, off Broadway productions by up and coming writers, that's great. There are cabaret rooms in London and New York where that would be perfect. Sing them there, and like Liz, you'll be lauded by the critics and adored by your fans. Sing them on a cruise ship to a family crowd, whose only experience of live theatre is 'Mamma Mia!', and you've had it. Theme your show by all means, but don't limit your options.

Steven Applegate is a musical director and arranger for such stars as Christine Aguilera and Idina Menzell. He says, "It seems that performers are so involved and concerned about creating a show around a specific theme or emphasis, that sometimes they forget about just entertaining."

He's right. There are exceptions, but you're in the entertainment business and your audience is there to be entertained. Paying audiences will be happy to indulge you to a point, but people celebrating a wedding or enjoying a cruise vacation don't want a history lesson or to be challenged with interesting chord progressions. They just want to hear songs they know, performed in a familiar way. They want to get to know you, hum along, then go to the buffet. That's it. If you're planning to use your show as a platform to educate the masses in musical appreciation, well... good luck.

This doesn't mean you need to sell-out and just sing tired old crowd-pleasers. Band leader Joey Mix says, "One of the complaints we have is that everyone seems to go for the most popular songs that will appeal to most of the people most of the time. I think it's good to throw in a curve ball here and there to try and surprise and educate the audience a little bit." There are thousands of hugely popular songs out there that also happen to be well written. Find the ones that mean something to you and your audience.

Lisa Cottrell thinks it's important to "select material that suits your voice and that you know you sing really well." She warns, "If you attempt a song just because it's the latest big hit, you really have to make sure you're bringing something new to it. You should sing it as well as, or even better than, the original."

If you're a production singer, hired to sing in someone else's show, you'll have no choice over the repertoire, the keys, the musicians, the lighting or what you say. One of the great advantages of having your own show is that you can sing and say what you like, how you like.

However you do it, your show must trigger an emotional response.

Find the emotional triggers

Music has the power to take us back in time and re-live key moments in our lives. I like to sing 'Moon River'. For me it's a pretty tune with nice words, but that's about it. To a couple in the audience who danced to that song at their wedding 25 years ago, it has a powerful emotional resonance. Maybe 'Unforgettable' was the favourite song of someone's late father or the first dance at a sister's wedding. Being able to move the audience and touch their hearts is what it's all about.

"Music is the soundtrack of our lives." Dick Clark

There is a wonderful charity called Playlist for Life that has embraced the remarkable power that music can have on people living with dementia. Hearing their favourite songs from decades ago can trigger joy and completely change their personality, if only for a moment. Such is the power of music, that doctors have begun prescribing it as part of the patients' care. When I find videos of these beautiful music moments I share them on the Cabaret Secrets Facebook group.

Research your audience to understand where you can find those emotional triggers. It's not difficult. We never forget the music we grow up with. If most of your audience is around 60 years old, you can be sure to stir a few memories by including hits from the 1970s. A quick Internet search shows they ranged from Barry Manilow's 'Mandy', Queen's 'Bohemian Rhapsody', and Glen Campbell's 'Rhinestone Cowboy'.

I also found the most popular songs played at weddings over the years include 'Love Me Tender', 'When You Say Nothing At All', 'Just The Way You Are' and 'Unchained Melody'. I like the way Jodi Picoult puts it in 'Sing You Home':

> Every life has a soundtrack. There is a tune that makes me think of the summer I spent rubbing baby oil on my stomach in pursuit of the perfect tan. There's another that reminds me of tagging along with my father on Sunday morning to pick up the New York Times. There's the song that reminds me of using fake ID to get into a nightclub; and the one that brings back my cousin Isobel's sweet sixteen, where I played Seven Minutes in Heaven with a boy whose breath smelled like tomato soup. If you ask me, music is the language of memory.

When a song makes an emotional connection it has a power all of its own. This is serious stuff. We're talking about the soundtrack of someone's life. Litter your set with songs like that and you're on to something special. Maria von Trapp said, "Music acts like a magic key, to which the most tightly closed heart opens."

Singer Neile Adams puts it like this:

Cabaret is an opportunity to share life at a direct, intimate and emotional level. Audiences recognise in the performer something of themselves through the songs performed. Indeed, although the experiences may vary, the emotions are almost always the same.

Pushing boundaries

Time Out London's Cabaret Editor, Ben Walters, thinks cabaret is at its best when it makes the audience think:

> Good cabaret should contain some element of progressive or provocative material - not necessarily with a desire to shock or scandalise but, like all art, to push audiences into challenging their thinking about whatever aspect of life the material of the show relates to.

I like that. We don't have to "shock or scandalise" just for the sake of it - sometimes it's enough to make an audience think, and as a result, we hope, make them grow a little. The most rewarding theatre I've seen has always stayed with me, changing me in some small way.

It's okay to push boundaries, but you need to know when to stop. Marta Sanders loves lively character songs which some people consider a little risqué. For years she thought these prudes needed to lighten up and she'd sing them regardless of who was in the audience. Then she realised she was being a little headstrong. She now realises:

> The point is not to cut somebody off. So I may feel that it's stupid that they can't just get it, and wonder why they're taking it so seriously, but the reality is that there are lot of people who do take things seriously. So what

I have learned, reluctantly, is that I do have to honour that.

She's right. During a run of Christmas shows at a sophisticated London cabaret room, some idiot took offence at a harmless comedy song called 'The Silly Slang Song'. In fact, the man was so offended (and drunk), he lobbed two heavy salt-cellars at me. Amazing. The story even turned up in the The Stage Newspaper:

> Gary Williams... found himself under fire during a recent gig at London's Pizza on the Park. Williams, who is probably best known for his appearances in the West End in The Rat Pack Live from Las Vegas, was in the middle of singing the Silly Slang Song when he was struck in the shin by a salt mill which had seemingly been flung by an audience member. Assuming the a-salt (apologies) was some kind of bizarre incident (perhaps someone throwing salt over their shoulder for good luck?), Williams persisted, before being struck again - this time in the stomach - during his encore. House lights were raised and the offender made himself known, claiming he had been insulted by the song because it was homophobic. Williams - openly gay himself - proceeded to introduce his partner on stage, provoking an apology of sorts from the man, who soon scarpered. "The guy must have been out of his mind," said Williams, "If one of the mills had hit someone in the head it could have caused serious injury or even worse. In all my years of performing, I've never seen anything like it - even at the rowdiest corporate events."

Published in The Stage Newspaper 7th January 2010

As you can see, in cabaret, you have to be ready for anything. Sometimes a real 'fourth wall' would be quite handy.

Summary
Finding your theme might take some time but the process is straightforward.

- Sing your favourite songs that suit your voice.
- Always look to make an emotional connection with your audience.
- Never alienate them.
- Don't get so focused on your theme you forget to entertain.
- Give the audience something to think about, challenge them in some small way.
- Keep it honest and real.
- If you open up and share something of yourself with the audience, they will do the same for you.

When it all comes together the effect is magical. On the other hand, if you get it wrong... be prepared to duck.

Secret 3: Be Sincere

In real life, most of us can spot a fake. None of us enjoy wasting our time with bullshitters. On the other hand, if someone is welcoming, friendly, genuine, revealing and receptive - we tend to respond in a similar way.

The energy we give off is infectious. Honestly begets honesty. If we are open with people, they'll be more open in return. Life's better that way, isn't it? I believe that what goes around comes around, and try to live by The Golden Rule 'Treat others as you would have them treat you.'

So what's all this got to do with being a performer? Everything.

We are communicators on a grand scale. If we love what we do, singing songs and sharing stories, the audience will respond. Our energy is infectious. If we feel good, so does everyone else and the energy multiplies.

Here then is one of the most important things I can tell you about performing. Be sincere.

> *"This above all: to thine own self be true," William Shakespeare, Hamlet*

Lennie Watts shared with me the kind of singers who've left an impression with him over the years:

> In all of my years working in cabaret, from bar-tending at Don't Tell Mama to opening and booking the

Metropolitan Room, the artistes that stick out to me are those who knew who they were, felt comfortable in their skin, and weren't afraid to be themselves. So many performers have some crazy notion of what they think it's all about. They become a totally different person when they step on stage. In an intimate cabaret setting, you can't get away with hiding. We can see you! Having a terrific voice is great, but we figure that out in the opening number... then where do you go?

Make a connection

Playing a part in a 'book show', where the score tells you what to sing and the director tells you where to stand is one thing, but that's not the business you're in. Being a cabaret artiste is all about breaking the fourth wall and making a connection with the audience through the power of our personalities. In this context I think that we're basically the same people on stage as we are off. For all the lighting effects, choreography and clever patter, our real personalities will always come through. There's nowhere to hide. If you're doing your job right you need to open up to complete strangers and trust they'll do the same for you.

Annemarie Lewis Thomas, Principal of musical theatre school The MTA, explained to me how she feels musical theatre and cabaret require completely different skill sets:

> Generally speaking musical theatre performers enjoy doing musical theatre because they can create a role and 'be' someone else for the duration of the show. In cabaret it's more about 'being' yourself. As we all know 'being' yourself is the hardest thing of all – let alone on stage in a vulnerable state. That's why we teach it as a module at The MTA – if nothing else for my students to revere the art of cabaret.

Steven Applegate told me, "The key to being a great performer is to tell the story. Every artiste has a responsibility to do just this. Without the story, who cares how beautiful you sound?"

Singer, Jan Abrams, loves the intimacy of cabaret, the storytelling through an hour of song. "In a way," she says, "it sort of reminds me of letting people into your living room. The cabaret performer is, after all, revealing a part of their life. It's often a vulnerable place to be, but it's honest and real, and, for me, beyond beautiful voices and beautiful songs."

Producer Gary England thinks successful cabaret is rooted in sincerity but warns artistes not to become too self-indulgent.

> I think cabaret is about being able to lay yourself bare and exposing who you really are in front of strangers. It's an art form in its own right. A good artiste needs to feel comfortable with a small audience and choose material that either has a narrative or tells a story. It's less about 'belting out standards' (we can go to concerts for that) and more about niche or new material. It can be funny, tragic or harrowing but it has to be sincere and make you feel something.
>
> Stand out performers include Kristen Chenoweth as part of the Donmar Diva Season who had exactly the right patter between songs - giving context without self indulgence. I loved Maria Friedman's one woman show where she laid her heart on the line and chose songs that told stories. With Maria it wasn't about her voice, it was about the story. So many artists ramble between songs and talk absolute rubbish. The best cabaret for me is scripted to the hilt with pace and rhythm. Seeing Elaine Stritch was a masterclass in storytelling and turning emotions on a penny - one minute you're laughing, the next crying. Ann Hampton

Callaway and Liz Callaway had great patter: playful, fun, and though scripted it felt completely natural. Too many artistes tend to indulge themselves and assume they're more entertaining when they're spontaneous and doing it 'on the hoof' but they simply aren't.

I've seen the biggest West End and Broadway stars absolutely bomb in cabaret when they have to be themselves and not a character.

We'll cover how to write and deliver an effective script in secret number five, but Gary's right about the importance of great patter (and he has a great name).

Opening yourself up to strangers can be intimidating. It requires a leap of faith and plenty of confidence, but I think it's worth the risks.

Now you understand the importance of sincerity, good preparation and choosing the right theme for your show, get a pen and plenty of paper... it's time to create your first running order.

Secret 4: Use A Template

Broadway star, recording artiste and cabaret master Liz Callaway told me, "I love interaction with the audience. It's strange because I used to find it very difficult looking at people when I performed, probably because I came from theatre where you have a spotlight on you and only see black. Now, I sometimes ask to have the house lights on so I can see who I'm singing to! At the end of a show, I like my audience to feel that, in addition to enjoying an evening of great music, they have had dinner with me."

I want to share with you the thoughts of singer Barbara Brussell, who picks up on that theme, and beautifully describes how an evening of cabaret should feel:

> Cabaret is live theatre... and, just like in life, anything can happen.
>
> I liken putting a cabaret show together to hosting a party. A diverse group of people are invited, and whoever decides to show up gathers together (sometimes knowing each other, often not), in a pleasing environment to spend a couple of pleasant hours away from home. They escape from life's routine and trust their host or hostess to provide an entertaining evening.
>
> Structuring a cabaret show resembles the natural progression of a party. Beginnings can be awkward. To help the guests feel comfortable in their new

environment, there is a ritual. You open the door, welcome them in, give them time to look around, offer them a drink, all helping them to get their bearings and feel at ease. When putting an act together we do the same thing with songs to help the audience relax and feel at ease. This order of presentation is important in building trust, nothing too jarring too early on. You wouldn't greet your guests, and serve them a filet mignon at the front door. The entree, the 'meat' of the evening, comes later, deeper in the arc of the night.

As the evening winds down and your guests must leave. Their hearts are a little fuller, minds a little richer, spirits uplifted and dreams rekindled. Now, that's a great meal!

Tara Khaler was an established production singer determined to put her own act together. Working in a show on a cruise ship gave her ready access to musicians, technicians and most importantly, a theatre with an audience. Even with all this it was a long process. It took Tara over a year of preparation and three complete performances in this relatively safe environment before she felt fully confident to go it alone. Check out Tara's interview on the Cabaret Secrets podcast.

Bit by bit, putting it together

Starting with a blank piece of paper can be daunting. There are so many choices it can be hard to know where to begin. Over the years I've developed a systematic way of creating a show from start to finish. Here are the four steps to take before you even think about warming up your voice:

- List all the songs in your repertoire
- Categorise your songs

- Choose a template
- Draft your first running order

1. List your songs

Make a list of all the songs you enjoy and sing well. All of them. This should be a big list. At least fifty songs, ideally a lot more. Keep the theme of your show in mind, but don't let it limit you too much just yet. At this stage just get as many song titles down as possible. Take Barbara Brussell's advice:

> Always have a way to write down songs that you might want to sing. Sometimes songs come into our heads, songs we didn't even know we knew. Follow them. If you love a song, don't let anyone tell you it isn't for you. Whether it's the melody, the rhythm, the lyric, or the message of the song, trust it and find a way to make it work for you.

2. Categorise your songs

Next put all your songs into categories relating to styles. Depending on your show, you might have a Broadway section, a pop section, or a section paying tribute to a particular composer. Some songs may fit in two categories, e.g. The Girl from Ipanema could go in 'Slow and Romantic' and 'Latin'. You should have a category for songs that make good 'openers' for your show. Here are some suggestions for category headings. Feel free to make your own, based on your repertoire.

- Fast and lively openers
- Medium
- Slow and romantic
- Dramatic
- Comedy and character

- Latin
- Broadway
- Swing
- Songs about American cities
- Songs that influenced me as a child
- Show-stoppers

Now you've listed and categorised all of your songs, you're ready for step 3: choosing a template. It's the key to saving a lot of time and effort.

3. Choose a template

Whether they realise it or not, most artistes follow a set of tried and tested rules when creating their shows. Understanding these rules will demystify the process and give you a basis from which to work. Here's what Kim Gavin told me about working with Take That:

> When I first started working with the band in the 1990s, I realised you can't just keep banging the audience with music and dance, you have to give them something else. Over the years we've found this formula that helps us to structure the shows. For example, there's always an 'opening' section where we wow everyone first with the theme and an exciting start to get them onboard, then, usually after three songs, we start talking to them. When we're in Scotland or Wales we get them to sing the national anthem, maybe Bread of Heaven or something like that.
>
> It's important you touch the people so they know you care about them. It all comes back to making a connection and this formula helps us get there.
>
> The last tour we did with the band was weird

because we were opening three times in the same show. First we had Take That 4, then Robbie came out, and finally That That 5. It threw the normal rule book out the window and everything got shifted around.

You do get some people coming to every single show who start to see the patterns, so we like to be as current as we can and keep it fresh.

In a moment I'll break down one of my shows and explain exactly how it's structured, why the songs are in that particular order and why I chat when I do. It's the structure we're interested in - at this stage the actual songs are incidental, it's what the songs are doing that's important.

Most shows can be broken down into a number of sections consisting of two, three or four songs relating to each other in some way. This is where using groups or 'sections' can be a great help in narrowing down which songs to include from the list you just made.

Give each section a theme so it becomes a sort of mini show in itself. Maybe you're telling the story of how you discovered music and began performing (the songs in this section could vary in style from rock to classical as you talk about what influenced you as a child), other sections could be swing tunes, songs from a particular country, or even from one period of a songwriter's career.

Grouping songs together like this helps when building your show because you can focus on perfecting each self-contained section at a time.

Having the sections themed also helps when deciding what to say to the audience. 'Patter' or 'chat' is the glue that binds your show together and provides an opportunity for the audience to get to know you.

The other nice thing about sections is that you can easily insert them or remove them from your show. This is especially handy if you need a shorter set. You'll save a lot of time just using two or three tried-and-tested sections, complete with the usual chat.

Here's the template I used for a season I did in Brazil. The show was for families on a cruise vacation, so I purposely kept the material mainstream and generally upbeat. Most of the guests were Brazilian and spoke only Portuguese so I spent months before the season learning their language - at least enough for the show. Remember the actual songs I chose are less important than the affect they had on the audience. We're really interested in what they contributed to the show. For example, were they 'up' (uptempo), ballads or character songs? The sections I used were:

- Opening
- Brazilian
- Spanish
- Final Build
- Finale

Opening Section. The opening and closing sections are the easiest to put together. I want to grab the audience's attention right at the top of the show then segue into something medium paced. This gives them a chance to get to know me and settle into the show. Then it's time to chat.

1. Short, lively opener: 'Coffee Song/Brazil Medley'
Your opening can be fast or slow. Ideally it will be well known, catchy and represent the flavour of your show. The first time you step on to the stage is always the most nerve-wracking, so this should be something you're very comfortable singing - a failsafe. You're working with unfamiliar lighting, trying to gauge your audience, hoping your mic will work and the band will play

well. There is a lot to think about. You need to be completely comfortable with this song, so you can be free to worry about all the other things happening around you. Remember what Barbara Brussell said - this is you opening the door to your dinner guests and welcoming them into your world. Just as you wouldn't open the door on a unicycle wearing a pink body stocking (or maybe you would), you probably shouldn't open your show with anything too shocking. Save that for later.

2. Medium tempo. Needs to connect: 'Can't Take My Eyes Off You'
I've made an impact with my opener, now it's time for the audience to relax and get to know me. They'll be deciding whether they like me or not, and frankly, I'll be doing the same with them. This is why I like my second number to have a relaxed feel so we can all get comfortable. Other than a quick "Hello and welcome to the show," I won't say much before this song.

   I chose 'Can't Take My Eyes Off You' because I know Brazilians love it, and it gives a great opportunity to get everyone involved. During the first chorus I come down from the stage and get the audience singing and clapping along. I might pose for photos, dance with someone or run all the way up to the back of the house. It's a great opportunity to put everyone in a relaxed, happy frame of mind, right at the top of the show.

3. Chat
This where I properly introduce myself to the audience. You should always be clear what you are trying to achieve each time you talk to your audience. Whatever you're saying should strengthen your connection with them and move things along. Now, near the top of the show, is your chance to gain their trust

and make friends.

Introduce yourself and give them an idea of what's in-store. Try adding a little self-deprecating humour, don't go on too long and remember: no one's come for a lecture in the history of music. Here's an example of the kind of thing I like to do::

> "Good evening everyone! Thank you for that warm welcome, I am so happy to be here with you tonight at Ronnie Scott's!
>
> [Reaction from the audience]
>
> This is of course the most stylish and discerning music venue in London, which must mean that right now, you are the most stylish and discerning people in London.
>
> [More reaction, then I would have the band start playing the intro to next song. The music helps to punctuate the chat, build the energy and subtly suggests to the audience that something is going to happen]
>
> One thing I've learned is to make the most of every moment we're given, and I know that we are going to have an incredible night tonight.
>
> [I say this to give a good energy to the audience and set up the Sinatra quote coming up]
>
> We've got some great music lined up for you tonight, including this, from the man who famously said, 'You've gotta love living baby, 'cause dying's a pain the arse,' the Chairman of the Board, Ol' Blue Eyes, Frank Sinatra."
>
> [Then I sing the song]

Even though I have done my act thousands of times, I still rehearse my opening chat before each performance. The audience may forgive mistakes later on, once I've proved myself, but the opening of the show has to be right.

We'll look in more detail at how to create a script for your show in secret number 5.

In this particular show it was important to sing the first two songs in English and not speak Portuguese. I wanted the predominantly Portuguese speaking audience to think I only spoke English. When I eventually talked to them in their language, they were delighted. It's all about expectations versus outcomes.

Brazilian Section. Four well-known songs, sung in Portuguese.

4. Ballad: 'The Girl From Ipanema'

Whatever ballad I choose needs to have a strong emotional resonance with the audience. In this case I went with 'The Girl From Ipanema' because it's part of Brazil's musical heritage and, for them, very evocative. For a British audience I might sing Matt Monro. Think of the kind of songs that will be a part of the audience's lives, the songs that might have been playing when they married or the first record they ever bought. Always try to make an emotional connection.

5. Medium: 'Samba Medley' with chat over vamp

I chat over the intro to this song about the music I enjoyed when I was growing up. It's quite personal and more engaging than just telling them when the song was written or how many copies it sold.

6. Up: 'Mas Que Nada' with band solos

I segue into another Brazilian favourite. There are band solos, which allow me to feature some of the musicians.

7. Up: 'Amigo'

Another well-known standard in Brazil.

Spanish Section. Here we have the tricky middle section. There's usually a section in everyone's show for random songs that don't really seem to fit anywhere else. You'll see this later when we look at how the stars do it. That said, in this show I got lucky. I found two popular Spanish songs that worked perfectly to connect me with the Spanish speakers in the audience. If you had lots of Germans in the house, you could sing two songs for them, or if you were on a ship you could reference one of the places you'd just visited.

8. Up: 'Amor'

9. Ballad: 'Perfidia'
Of course, it helps when a song is well known internationally, like Perfidia.

The Final Build. These songs build to the finale. There doesn't need to be a strong theme in this section, the priority is to build the mood and energy. I always look for a bam, Bam, BAM! ending. I want three big show-stoppers that take the show to a crescendo: big, bigger, biggest! No chat in between. This section is about drive, dynamism and emotion. They don't all have to be fast songs, as long as they are powerful and well known.

Veronica Ferriani uses this technique in her show. Her last three songs are the most popular crowd-pleasers she knows, but still there's a personal touch. First she steps into the house singing a very sentimental ballad that every Brazilian knows and loves to sing. Then she picks up the tempo with a lively samba that's all about endings (one of the lines is, "I must go, my mother is waiting for me at home.") and finally she closes the show with a joyous, upbeat song.

10. Up: 'Copacabana'

11. Up: 'That's Life'

12. Audience Interaction: 'Strangers In The Night'
Using a ballad here is an odd choice, but it's what I do with the song that makes it work. I go into the audience, handing out flowers while they take pictures. The energy builds not because of the tempo but because of the audience interaction, which makes that all important connection. I'd been doing this 'business' for years all over the world, but found by accident that Roberto Carlos, a big star in Brazil, also does the same thing. When the audience saw me doing it, they thought it was in homage to him, one of their heroes, which further endeared me to them.

When I returned for my second season in Brazil I made a few changes to this show. Instead of hitting them with 'That's Life' I set a romantic mood with 'When I Fall In Love', and then replaced 'Strangers' with Louis Armstrong's 'Wonderful World'. Though I still gave out the flowers, the audience was markedly more reserved. No longer were ladies screaming at me with outstretched arms from the balconies (this happened most weeks), now they just smiled at me, politely hoping I'd hand them a rose. Building into 'Strangers' with a lively song energised the audience, whereas the Nat Cole ballad killed the energy, making everyone sit back and relax. It's a good example of how one song can have a strong impact on the shape of the show.

Finale Section. Having built the excitement up in the previous section, it's important to close the show on a high.

13. Up: 'New York, New York'

14. Chat
I thank audience, introduce 'My Way' and subtly suggest it might be the last song.

15. Dramatic ballad: 'My Way' + bows
Over the years I've given a lot of thought to the best way to close a show. There are three choices: a fast, fun, happy-clappy song (e.g. a rock 'n' roll medley); a tender, romantic ballad that makes the audience feel sentimental (e.g. 'Somewhere Over the Rainbow', 'The Party's Over' or 'Time To Say Goodbye'); or a big, dramatic ballad that triggers an emotion (e.g. 'I Will Always Love You', 'A Song For You', 'Nessun Dorma', 'If I Never Sing Another Song').

My preference is the dramatic ballad. People love big notes and drama. If you can also pull at their heart strings all the better.

Many of these songs are over-done (I avoided 'My Way' for years) but remember, most people rarely hear them live on stage. You may get sick of singing them and the band may roll their eyes at your lack of originality, but don't let the popularity of a song put you off.

If you're prone to turn your nose up at popular songs just because they're popular, here's what the world's most successful songwriter, Irving Berlin, had to say, "Listen kid, take my advice. Never hate a song that's sold half a million copies". . .

16. Chat
It's time for some final thank-yous, a quick joke, then "one more".

This is how I like to close my shows. The chat has three clear parts: thank-yous, a joke, and "Would you like one more?"

Thanking the audience is a nice thing to do, but I don't usually thank all of the technical staff after each show. On most ships, at least, the cruise director will come on stage after you and thank them anyway. Besides, you'd never hear a big star thanking their lighting guy from the stage. Just buy them a beer after the show. Believe me, they'll appreciate that a lot more than a scripted thank you.

17. Up: "Gipsy Kings Medley" + bows
I finished with a lively medley because Brazilians like to party. For more reserved audiences, I might just end with 'My Way'.

The benefits of using a template
This particular template was to prove useful sooner than I expected. I was asked to go back and perform a second season in Brazil. I knew many of the guests would be repeat cruisers so I had to make a few changes. Instead of having to start from scratch and rethink the whole show, I just replaced some of the songs in this template with similar alternatives. I replaced 'Girl from Ipanema' with 'Quiet Night of Quiet Stars' and 'Mas Que Nada' with 'Samba de Orfeu'. Again, it's not the actual song that important, it's the mood it creates and how it helps to shape the show.

How much material do you need?
You could be asked to perform for as little as 15 minutes or as much as two hours. For corporate events, and some private parties, less is more. If the guests are not expecting any entertainment and are there to enjoy the wine and conversation, you've got your work cut out. All you can do is grab their attention in the first few seconds and not let them go till you're done. 15-20 minutes of high impact material is usually enough for this sort of crowd.

Cabaret rooms, where people are paying to hear you sing, sometimes ask for a single 60 minute set but usually they want two sets of around 45-60 minutes each. Some cruise ships only need one 50 minute show, others require two. Usually they'll ask for one full show and up to 30 minutes more for a 'split show' with another entertainer. To sum up, you should really have at least two different 45 minute shows, with plenty of spares to hand.

Look to the stars
There's no getting away from templates but don't just take my word for it. Interested to learn how my approach compared with other artistes and curious to see if any patterns emerged, I analysed live concerts of Michael Bublé, Matt Monro, Amy Winehouse and Celine Dion. I was surprised to see just how much they all have in common.

Turn to the appendix to see the analyses for yourself. Like me, you'll discover tried and tested rules that work, regardless of decade or genre. I found how the opening section always sets the mood for the evening. For example, Michael Bublé and Celine Dion used a dramatic ballad to seize the audience's attention. Everyone else went straight in with a lively, punchy song.

There's always a tricky middle section where everyone seems to use the songs that don't really belong anywhere else. There's no strong theme here so it is a good place to try songs that are a little different, that stand on their own. I sometimes sing a different song in this part of the show every night. It's a place to play, where I might allow myself to be a little indulgent.

The build towards the end of the show is always three big, strong, lively songs (bam, Bam, BAM!) and everyone includes some kind of audience participation.

The finale is either a big dramatic ballad (Celine Dion, Michael Bublé and Matt Monro), or something lively (Amy Winehouse). I used both - a false tabs with 'My Way' followed by 'The Gypsy Kings Medley' as an encore.

4. Draft your first running order

You're now ready to put your first running order together. Once you've looked over the templates used by the stars you'll have a good idea of where to start. Choose a template that best matches your musical style and use it as the basis for your first running order.

Let me say again, we're not interested in the actual songs the artiste chose - it's the type of song and what it did for the show that's important.

Let the template guide you. If you need a short lively opener, simply go down your repertoire list and choose one. As your show begins to take shape and you need something a little different, just go back to your list.

You should change the section names to those more suitable for your act. Instead of Michael Bublé's 'Sinatra' section, yours might be 'Frank Loesser' or 'Fred Astaire'.

Don't get bogged down in details just yet, you won't get it right first time. Get your first running order together quickly so you have something to build on.

If you can, make a playlist of your show on your computer so you can listen to the whole thing from start to finish. Get a feel for the shape of the show, the segues, where you can talk and how it builds. Using a computer playlist is a great way to experiment. It will also give you an idea of how long the show will run, and whether or not you have enough material.

Summary

Think of your show like hosting a dinner party for friends. Welcome them into your home and carefully serve each course to build the mood and energy of the evening.

List all your best songs then learn how the stars structure their shows to inspire your first template.

As your show takes shape you'll need to think about how to

link your songs and sections together. It's time to look at how to talk to an audience.

Secret 5: How To Chat To An Audience (and not sound like a fake)

Whether you're addressing a business meeting, giving a speech at a wedding, or singing on a cruise ship, talking to a crowd is something many of us struggle with. In speaking to dozens of cabaret experts for this book, everybody stressed how important good 'chat' or 'patter' is to a successful cabaret.

A great voice is not enough

Singer, Jeff Harnar, has definite opinions about the importance of patter:

> It's in the patter between the songs where an artiste can make or break the show. Having an exceptional voice is essential for recitals or certain theatrical roles, but cabaret is about intimacy.
>
> What sets cabaret singers apart is the connection they craft with both words and songs. It's about creating a relationship with the audience that feels present, authentic, and worthy of holding their attention for an hour.
>
> I've found having a director hugely helpful in keeping me 'on pitch' with my patter. I've seen many artistes undermine the goodwill they've established

with their vocals with their words in between.

Big band singer, Eleanor Keenan says:

> Learn to love interacting with the audience. You don't have to be the best singer in the world, but a bit of charm goes a long way. Whatever you say must be sincere. You must feel it or they won't believe it.

Mark Shenton agrees:

> The key to all of the great cabaret singers is that, as well as performing the songs, they offer something more, either of themselves and/or about the material. Great patter is essential to achieve this. No gushing phoney sentiment; just something that truly contextualises why they are here and why you should be here, too.
> Keep your patter crisp, informative, and sincere. There is nothing I hate more than phoney patter.

I like that. Remember secret number 3? Be Sincere. It matters in everything you do, but especially when you are talking to an audience.

Cruise Directors see literally hundreds, if not thousands of entertainers: the good, the bad, and the terrible. João Wolf told me, "I've seen people who are not good at talking trying to chat to the audience and boring them so much, that by the time they get to the song itself, they'd lost interest."

That won't surprise Lisa Cottrell. She's found that chat is something many singers struggle with:

> Some singers, particularly those from a musical theatre background, find it difficult to 'be themselves' on stage.

This is a common problem for trained musical theatre singers as they're used to playing a role. For them, being asked to chat in a relaxed manner to an audience is very alien. In fact, a lot of performers are attracted to the stage precisely because it offers the opportunity to 'be someone else'. Often they can actually be quite shy in their normal life, away from the stage.

That's something Annemarie Lewis Thomas knows well:

Patter in between the songs is what our musical theatre students struggle with the most. Whilst I appreciate that some cabaret performers just segue from song to song, on our module they learn how to write and deliver the patter too. It's terrifying as it's so exposing.
It's always the same too – the people that consider themselves naturally funny struggle at first, whilst the more reserved ones really shine.

Watch the Tony Award winning 'Elaine Stritch At Liberty' to see how one musical theatre star conquered cabaret. It's a tightly scripted, heavily directed show but she brings such sincerity and pathos to every performance.

Practise and experience
Tara Khaler describes chat as, "the glue for the show". She says she can stand up and sing for hours on end. "I know a million songs, but to create a show you need to have a good directorial sense and know how to paint a picture. It's hard to come up with chat that's genuine and worth saying, but it does get easier with experience."

To hear a perfectly executed script, check out the legendary Marlena Shaw's recording of 'Go Away Boy', where she holds the audience in the palm of her hand. That sort of command doesn't just happen overnight. She told me she felt the fear and said it anyway: "I got comfortable with my audience when I stopped being afraid of them. Life experience helps a lot too - the more I've done, the more I've got to say."

I know that's something Lisa Cottrell would agree with:

> Chatting with ease to an audience is something that comes with experience. The ability to connect with the demographic and judge the room is quite a talent in itself.
>
> A cruise ship audience is particularly difficult where age and nationality play a big part. The main skill is in the delivery and timing.
>
> I tell my singers to talk 'to' the audience, not 'at' them and try to make friends with them. The goal is to leave the audience with the feeling that they got to know you a little bit.

Nothing's as easy as it looks

After seeing a polished performer, people will often tell them, "Oh, chat's easy for you, you've just got the gift of the gab." They don't see the hours of practice it takes to make it look so natural. The same applies to anyone at the top of their game. As a young athlete Mo Farah learned from his heroes. "They run, sleep, train and that's it," he said. "I'm living my life in that manner now. I realised that if I was going to have a chance, I needed to live like they did, completely dedicated." Likewise, footballer Leo Messi said, "I trained 17 years to be an overnight success."

Fred Astaire didn't just slip on a pair of dance shoes and create the choreography for 'Top Hat' in ten minutes. He practised so hard his feet would bleed. But who wants to know that? As an audience we want to believe it all just happens, as if by magic.

That's showbiz! When it's done well it should look easy. If it looks hard, something's wrong.

Watch Frank, Dean and Sammy fooling around in those old 'Rat Pack' shows. You'd swear they're just making it all up as they go along: three guys, sipping bourbon, happy to share a joke with the audience. That's the magic. The reality is that all of those routines were written, crafted and rehearsed.

This time it's personal

We often think of cabaret as being reserved to intimate lounges, but that doesn't have to be the case. At its heart, cabaret is about connecting with people. Kim Gavin's worked on huge concert tours with Take That and thinks making that personal connection is key to any artiste's success, however large the venue. As you'll see, it's what's in the "gaps" that makes the magic:

> One show that had no connection or interaction with the audience was a Michael Jackson concert. Yes, there were lots of screens and pyros and amazing lighting effects, but he hardly said a word. The only thing that he actually said was, 'I love you'.
>
> There are a lot of stadium fillers out there who can't talk to an audience. The thing I've always done with Take That is include lots of chat. Gary Barlow's always very comfortable on stage and Robbie Williams is a real natural who always tries to get right to the back of the room. For example, he'll see someone leaving and he'd say, 'That girl with the black dress, holding the red handbag,' she turns around and suddenly he's got the whole audience with him.
>
> There are naturals and non-naturals, but the more you rehearse the better you get. It just takes time. It's about each singer finding their style and what works

for them.

If Robbie's doing a big show, he's not usually worried about the songs, he's looking at what he's doing in between the songs. That's his concentration. He surprised us all on the last tour because he looked like he wasn't really prepared. He'd say, 'I might do that bit there, but let's just see what comes,' but we knew as soon as he got on stage that he'd actually worked at all the links. He'd worked hard on the gaps so he could ad-lib and make it all sound more natural. You can only do that when you're in a comfortable place.

Having worked with some of the great singers like Whitney Houston, Natalie Cole and Sammy Davis Jr, Musical Director Barry Robinson knows the importance of a good set-up. He told me:

> The cardinal sin is cliché ridden introductions, like 'This is a beautiful song...', 'I hope you like my version of...', and 'It goes something like this...' Make the links interesting; personalise them. Maybe there's a story attached to the song or a special reason you're performing it. Sammy Davis was the master of this. He would set the scene so perfectly that the audience was mesmerised before the song had even started.

No one's born with the ability to tell anecdotes in front of 800 strangers with a spotlight burning into their face. When it doesn't come naturally, many just give up.

It takes a lot of time and practice to make something look easy. I (just about) know what I'm doing, but still, I know that every new script I need to memorise is going to need a lot of time and commitment.

Learning to be yourself on stage, to talk to an audience in a relaxed and natural way, takes time and experience, but there are practical things you can do to speed up the process. I promise, with a little time and effort, anyone can do it.

Let's look at how to script a show based on four different types of 'chat', the golden rule of respecting other performers, and how to hold the attention of everyone in the room.

The Four Different Types of Chat

Don't know what to say? Here's some practical advice on how to start scripting your show. I divide chat into four types: information, personal anecdotes, famous anecdotes and comedy.

1. Information

The easiest and most predictable chat is information: who arranged the song, the album it came from, when the composer was born and so on. A little of this can be useful, but be careful, too many facts can get boring.

Cabaret doyen Steve Ross suggests following Sinatra's lead. "Don't struggle with patter," he told me:

> It doesn't *have* to be ripped from the pages of your life! You don't have to tell us who recorded each song or made it famous. Sinatra never gave any biographical information, but he would refer to the composers and arrangers, so you can always fall back on that. I suggest you share your observations about the music, how you connect to it emotionally and what drew you to it in the first place.

If you're giving information, embellish it with a story. The audience doesn't just want to learn something, they want to feel something.

Whenever I hear someone say (in a clearly scripted voice), "Thank you very much ladies and gentlemen. In 1969 Dustin Hoffman wowed the critics with his performance in the now classic movie Midnight Cowboy. Here's the famous theme from that wonderful film," my inner voice screams "Boring!" Who cares? It's dull, and it's lazy. Now tell me bit of gossip about Dustin Hoffman or John Voight and I might be a bit more interested. Tell me a funny anecdote about the film and I'm entertained. Remember, you're not giving a lecture and no one wants a history lesson.

Hired to do a show for a French audience, Marta Sanders arrived at the venue to find another artiste had already performed one of her favourites, 'Autumn Leaves'. Her alternative was 'Annie's Song' but she couldn't think of anything to say to make it relevant to the audience. She took advice from a friend... and lied: "When John Denver went to Paris for the very first time with his wife, he fell in love with Paris and he fell even more in love with her... 'You fill up my senses...'" Much better. I wouldn't recommend telling too many lies in your show, but if you must, make sure they're good ones!

"That's what show business is, sincere insincerity." Benny Hill

Rather than just dates and names, give each song a set up with a personal edge. Marta says, "Look at what was going on in the songwriter's life at that time and make it personal, even gossipy. So rather than saying, 'This song was written by Cole Porter in 1952 for the musical 'Can Can', say, 'This was a time in Cole Porter's life when he felt the world was turning against him. He'd lost his fortune, his wife and his last musical was a flop. In his suite at the Waldorf in New York, he sat at his piano, and wrote this...' or, 'He'd just lost his mother and was sitting in his chair wondering what to do with his life and he wrote this...'

One of the best examples of this I've heard is from Michael Feinstein. The Gershwin standard 'Love Is Here To Stay' is a fixture in many cabaret sets.

Written by George and Ira Gershwin for the movie 'The Goldwyn Follies of 1938', it appeared in the 1951 MGM picture 'An American in Paris', and in 1995's 'Forget Paris'. It was originally called 'It's Here to Stay', then 'Our Love Is Here to Stay', but was finally published as 'Love Is Here to Stay'.

That's all very interesting, but there's another story. This was the last composition George Gershwin completed. Shortly after, in 1937, he died from a brain tumour, aged just 38. Ira was devastated and wrote the words for the song after his brother's death, giving the song a special poignancy.

Avoiding plain facts and figures, Feinstein shares with the audience the heartbreaking story of a brother's grief. By immersing us in their friendship and remarkable working relationship, the lyrics take on a whole new meaning and we feel something, we're moved. Now, whenever I hear, "It's very clear, our love is here to stay, not for a year, but ever and a day," I don't think of two lovers, I think of the love from one brother to another, and Ira's devastating loss.

2. Personal anecdotes

We've all got a few stories we like to tell. The kind of anecdotes you tell at a party to make your friends laugh, or maybe a well rehearsed answer when people ask, "How did do you become a singer?" Think what stories you have and write them down. Don't worry at this stage whether they're right for your show, just put everything down on paper.

Maybe you remember the day you bought your first record or the time you met one of your heroes after standing in the rain for hours. Maybe an airline lost your bags leaving you with no stage clothes. Perhaps you won a talent competition; your music teacher was a great mentor; or you arrived late for an audition, but got the job anyway. Maybe you discovered a particular artiste in an unusual way or someone left you money so you could buy your first piano. Think. They don't have to be groundbreaking stories.

Iain Mackenzie says, "Believe in what you're doing. If you're 100% committed to your performance the audience will follow," and singer Michael Dore agrees: "Be yourself. I think when people come to see you in cabaret they want a little insight into who you really are. Everyone loves gossip, inside stories and background information. I like to share things that relate to my life and career. A bit of name dropping never hurts either!"

"Everyone loves gossip" Michael Dore

Some acts like to include very personal stories about the day their first child was born, how the loss of their mother affected them, how their heart goes out to the victims of a recent tragedy or how they appreciate the brave soldiers fighting in faraway countries. They can be effective, but a word of warning. If you are going to use them, your delivery had better be perfectly sincere, otherwise, it's just cheap schmaltz reeking of opportunism. There are definite cultural differences here between American and British audiences. I truly mean no offence, but Americans tend to love this kind of heart-on-the-sleeve, apple pie, God Bless America stuff. The British just can't take it seriously. As the Americans are reaching for their tissues, the Brits are waiting for the punchline. By all means use this kind of sentimental chat, but only if you really mean it, and it comes from a place of genuine sincerity. When it's done right it can be very moving.

3. Famous anecdotes

Marta Sanders told me that chat is a key part of her shows and she never stops looking for something new to say. "I've been writing on napkins all of my life, collecting stories, songs and jokes from TV shows, other artistes and even witty quotes from daily calendars." She keeps them all in a book, and when she needs to write a link for a show she's sure to find some inspiration there. Once she's found what she's looking for, she writes it out then cuts it in half and then half again. "There should not", she says, "be a wasted word, ever."

Become a collector, like Marta. Research your material. Search the Internet, read biographies and always keep an ear out for anecdotes and one-liners already out there that you can use in your show. For example, when researching a Nat 'King' Cole tribute show, I found a nice story about one of his early gigs before he was known as a singer:

> One night a tipsy customer asked Nat to sing a song. He said no, but the customer insisted, so he sang it. The customer was so impressed he tipped the guys 15 cents and asked for another song. When Nat refused, the customer asked for his money back.

That's a nice story. It won't bring the house down, but it's amusing and sets up a Nat Cole song nicely. I don't have to follow it with, "And now here's a song by the great Nat 'King' Cole," there's no need. Tell the story, get the laugh and sing the song. It works beautifully, and I didn't even have to write it.

There are thousands of stories out there just like that one - some poignant, some funny, some long, some short. Write them down, keep them safe and one day you'll find the perfect place to use them.

4. Comedy

It's nice to sprinkle your show with a few laughs. Telling jokes 'stand up' style, might not be right for you or your show, but there are other ways. You could sing a comedy song or rework a stock gag, making it all about you or one of your musicians.

Comedian John Martin offers some serious advice to singers who want to be funny:

> A joke has to fit the person, or it won't sound right. You wouldn't wear shoes that are the wrong size, so why tell jokes that don't fit you? Some singers (and comedians) don't hear the joke, they just hear the laugh, and think, 'I'll use that' without understanding the principles and mechanics of the gag or considering whether or not it's right for them. There's absolutely nothing wrong with a singer telling a joke as long as it fits them. It's exactly the same with comics who sing songs that don't fit them. Everything has to be appropriate.

I agree. It took me years to find the kind of 'lines' that work for me, that suit my personality. Like John says, I'd hear a funny line somewhere and try it out myself, only to find it just wouldn't sit right. I am not a 'gag man'. I do better with gentle, self-effacing story-telling that's tightly woven into my act. If they happen to be true stories, even better.

I was once chatting to some guests on a ship who, not realising I was the singer, told me to my face that they walked out of my show and went to bed instead. I love that story and I've been telling it to friends for years. One day someone said I should include it in my show. I did, and it's become a fixture, always getting a great laugh.

On the very first cruise ship I worked on, a very nice elderly lady approached me, just as I walked off stage. "What a wonderful show," she said, "and your voice! Such a lovely tone. I could listen to you all day." I was flattered. I thanked her and asked, "Are you enjoying your cruise?" She just stared at me. I tried again, "I was wondering, are you enjoying your cruise?" Finally she said, "I'm sorry, you'll have to speak up, I'm profoundly deaf."

Funny, and I didn't even have to make it up. Sometimes I'll take a gag I like and reword it so it's a better fit for me. There's a line about an old man flirting with young woman. He says, "Where have you been all my life?" and she replies, "For most of it I wasn't even born." Rather than saying, "There was this old man chatting to a young woman..." I might say, "As you can see, our drummer is the oldest member of the band but that doesn't stop him flirting with just about every young woman he meets. Just today, after our sound check, I overheard him asking the girl who works in the box office..."

Be warned though, just because something gets a laugh, it doesn't mean it's appropriate. If I walked on stage without my trousers, people would laugh. But where's the craft in that? I remember once seeing a singer who had everyone in the palm of her hand with her wonderful voice. She could switch from opera to rock to jazz with remarkable ease. She was very natural with the audience but her jokes were crude. They cheapened her whole act. Yes, she was getting laughs, but at what price? Any sense of style or sophistication she'd established was lost in a moment.

Follow John's advice. Find ways to incorporate humour that fit you, your personality and your act.

The rule of threes

Don't ask me why, but if you want to build tension, get more applause, and live longer, three is a magic number. The rule of threes says that three things are better than two, five, and any other number. Threes are inherently funnier, more pleasing and generally more effective.

Over the band introduction to one of the songs in my Latin show, I say, "Tell me by applause how many of you here tonight like the music of Luis Miguel... The Gipsy Kings... and Roberto Carlos?"

For a Brazilian audience, each name I give is better known than the last. By the time I say, "Roberto Carlos" the audience is primed and responds with huge applause. The energy would be quite different if I just said, "Tell me by applause how many of you here like the music of Luis Miguel... and Roberto Carlos?"

The first two things you say set up a pattern that the third thing either complements or, if you're making a joke, derails.

Producer Clive Thomas tells everyone, "I like my audiences to be good looking, intelligent and slightly drunk... I suppose one out of three isn't bad."

Think about that next time you're eating a three course meal, reading the Three Little Pigs or listening to The Three Degrees.

Ad-libbing

You write your script and learn it by heart, but what if something happens in a show and you want to ad-lib? Cabaret Editor of Time Out London, Ben Walters, thinks freedom to go with the flow is a part of what makes cabaret special:

> For me, the crucial ingredient of cabaret is spontaneity. A cabaret show isn't just a transaction - an audience paying to be entertained - but a collaboration, or even a conspiracy, between everyone in the room. The performer leads things, of course, but everyone matters, everyone can make eye contact and the results will be unique to that event. A performer can (and

should!) prepare his or her material, but the true cabaret experience can't be rehearsed.

Paul L. Martin believes that cabaret is, "a dialogue with your audience." He told me:

> You have to riff off the vibe in the room. That means, despite all the preparation and rehearsal, always being prepared to throw the script or running order out of the window at a moment's notice.

And, Marta Sanders puts it like this:

> If you're going to speak, there's got to be a reason that you are speaking. The songs you're tying together are going to have cohesiveness because of what you say. The patter has to be very concise. There has to be a reason for saying every last word. It's okay to ad-lib but you must have a structure to rely on and to come back to.

I couldn't agree more. One of the great attractions to cabaret for the performer and the audience, is that anything can happen. It's in the spirit of the genre to ad-lib and go with a moment, but your script should never be too far away.

Write your own script

Whether it's personal information, an anecdote or comedy, the next step is to write a script. Choose your favourite gags, facts and stories from your lists and write them out in full, just as you would tell them. Punctuate each one just the way you would say it out loud.

Learn them by heart, and practice them over and over again.

Imagine the audience sitting there as you say the words out loud. Imagine their reaction and add pauses and laughs as if responding to them. As you keep going over them, refine them, improve them and update them. Practise the stories on your friends by just dropping them into everyday conversation, and continue refining them. If you're from a theatre background working with a script like this will be a familiar process.

Eventually you'll find the right 'shape' to your patter so the punchline or the song you're setting up has the strongest impact. Liz Callaway gave me some good advice

> Use your patter to gently lead your audience into the song but don't tell the whole story before you sing it. In other words, don't give the song away too early. Look for chances to surprise them.

It's so important that you make your script sound natural and conversational. You might add the odd "um" and "err" in there, and the occasional pause (don't over do it) just as you would in a real conversation. I prefer to hear this than a perfectly delivered 'voice over' style speech.

Think back to Barbara Brussell's dinner party. If you were chatting to one of your guests and they told you a story that sounded tired and rehearsed, you'd lose interest. You might even feel insulted. Exactly the same applies in your show. You should sound like you're telling your story to a small group of friends at a party for the first time. Look at how stand up comedians work. They feel it every time, and consequently, you do too.

Brazilian singer Veronica Ferriani finds it hard to repeat her script word-for-word and still sound natural. "That's doesn't work for me," she said, "Sometimes I wish it did, because I'd have less chance to make a mistake! For me, it's the idea that important, not the exact words. I know roughly what I'm going to say and where I am leading, but I use different words each time."

However you do it, remember what Eleanor Keenan said, "You must feel it, or they won't believe it." Take a moment to think about that. It's so important and one of the keys to your success as a cabaret artiste.

As soon as you're ready, start to incorporate your stories into your shows. Practise your script as often as possible - I can't stress this enough. The more you practise the more you'll find the rhythm and shape of each story. You'll know where to pause and what to emphasise to get the best reaction. Eventually they'll become second nature and an integral part of the section for which they were created.

On focus

When you're performing, especially if you're talking, all eyes are on you. If something else happens - a phone rings, a waiter drops a glass or someone throws a salt cellar at you - the audience's focus will shift. You can't let that happen for long. When something else catches everyone's attention, either acknowledge it and have fun with it, or simply look in the opposite direction, away from the distraction. The audience will follow your eyes, and you've reclaimed their focus. It works both ways: if you want the audience to look at a musician playing a solo - just look at the musician playing the solo. Their focus will follow yours.

Respect your colleagues

Stealing other people's material is out of the question. When you see another artiste do something that would be a good fit for your show, it can be tempting to steal it, but unless it's unique to that artiste, don't. You will be found out and soon get yourself a bad name in the business.

"Thou shall not steal" God

There is of course lots of material that's public domain. There are well known anecdotes like the Nat Cole one I mentioned, and of course lots of 'stock' gags that everyone's been doing for years. These are yours for the taking, but be aware that context should still be respected. For example, an artiste may use a famous anecdote to link two particular songs together or a series of short one-liners that help to build a theme. In this case, though the material is public domain, the way the artiste is using it is their own, and that should be respected. Imagine how frustrated you'd be if you'd spent years perfecting a ten minute section of your show and then found that someone saw it, stole it and got the credit for it.

Besides, creating your own script and routines (known as 'business') is a lot more fun than nicking someone else's. It's been said that stealing from one person makes you a thief but stealing from many makes you an innovator. Find inspiration in other acts (let's call it research) and create something special that's yours alone.

Summary

I asked Michael Feinstein how he learned to become a master of patter:

> The best way to become comfortable talking to an audience is to do it a lot. Practise is the only way to figure out what works and what doesn't. Eventually, somewhere along the way, you develop a style of your own.
>
> I was so lucky to work for five hours a night in a piano bar. That taught me how to engage a group and draw them in. Finding something that people can relate

to is important.

When I talk about a songwriter, it is for the purpose of putting them and their songs in a context that people can relate to today. With a little effort, there's always a way to find a bridge. It's often personality that sells a song more than vocal ability.

The key to good patter is sincerity. Keep it real, and follow these simple steps:

- Think of your own anecdotes and write them down.
- Research your subject and become a collector. Write down any interesting facts and well known stories you find.
- Only use humour that's a good fit for you and your show.
- Rehearse your new anecdotes and stories out loud. As you improve them, update your script.
- Practise them on your friends, in front of the mirror, in the car.
- Practise them again, and again, until they are second nature.
- Be inspired by other people's material and routines but don't rip them off. If in doubt, remember the Golden Rule: treat others as you would wish to be treated yourself.

I'm going to leave the last word on this chapter to Lennie Watts, who sums it up perfectly:

> Stay honest and tell your stories. I have a little thing I refer to that I call 'The F*#k it Factor'. That means 'let it go'! What's the worst thing that can happen? That's what I say to myself right before I go on stage. Be brave, tell the truth, and sing it like you wrote it! Don't strive for perfection, strive to be present and alive in each moment!

Secret 6: Live Performance Can Seriously Damage Your Health (and Ego)

The fourth wall, theatre's invisible barrier between you and your audience. While most actors are trained to observe that wall at all costs, as cabaret singers, it's our job to dismantle it and get down and dirty in the laps of our audience. Ben Walters says, "Cabaret makes eye contact. There's no fourth wall here - performers can see and hear you and will let you know it. The word 'cabaret' means 'room': what happens in a show depends on the dynamic between the performer and the audience in that place on that night. This is not television!" Indeed not.

The rules and pitfalls of audience participation
I'll never forget doing a corporate in Jersey walking around the tables crooning 'Everybody Loves Somebody', looking for a nice lady to dance a few bars with. Spotting just the one, I offered my hand and asked her up. "No, no," she said, "I can't dance." "Of course you can dance!" I said, getting everyone else to give her an encouraging round of applause as I took her hand. "No, no, really I can't," she protested, but I took her hand anyway and started to forcibly pull her up from her seat. "No!" she said, as her eyes bore into mine, "I can't dance. I'm disabled." At this point I had two choices: gently lower her back to her seat and publicly apologise, or ignore her and carry on. To my shame, I

chose the later. Having dragged her to her feet I had to sing the rest of the verse with her arms clasped around my neck, holding on for dear life. Served me right.

In other moments of doomed audience interaction I have been told to "f#@k off" (by a representative of the Arts Council no less), had missiles thrown at me, and had my innards torn out and fed to rabid dogs. The last one's actually a metaphorical description of an incident in 1990 when members of the Liberal Club in Scunthorpe didn't take to my Alec Wilder medley.

Once, at Ireland's National Concert Hall while singing Dean Martin's 'Volaré', I decided to kneel on the stage in a rash gesture of ardor, and hold my arm out towards a sweet old lady on the front row. She, with bandaged legs, returned the gesture by grabbing one of her crutches and pointing it towards me. It just reached. So there I am, singing a Neapolitan love song, holding the rubber stopper on the end of an Irish nana's NHS crutch. "What would Dean Martin do?" I thought. Have a drink, probably.

Recently, I saw a South American gaucho make an impressive demonstration with his bolas - you know, those weighted balls on long strings that spin around and clack on the stage in time to the music. To show how hard it was to master, and for the pure amusement of watching a member of the audience embarrass themselves, he got a female volunteer on stage, gave her a quick lesson, handed her the bolas, and said, "Have a try, let's see how well you do." Unfortunately for him, she did rather well. Out of an audience of 700 people he'd managed to pick another bolas expert. What are the chances? To the audience's delight she spun both balls around faster and in better time than the gaucho, who could do nothing but stand aside, grinning through gritted teeth.

My dad told me a similar story about a comic he saw, who got a fella who'd been heckling him all night, up on stage, and left him alone with a microphone, saying, "I know you think this job's easy, so let's see if you can do any better." Well as it turned out, he could. After five minutes of brilliant jokes the audience was howling with laughter. The comic had to return to the stage and somehow, resume control. I bet he thought twice before trying that again.

Sometimes the audience can participate in a show without even realising. I remember one performance of 'What Kind of Fool Am I?' when the lights dimmed, the room hushed, and as the band waited for me to sing the first line you could hear a pin-drop. Then, just as I drew breath, the magic was broken by a loud "Beep…beep…beep." We all looked up wondering where the noise was from coming from. Then I realised. An elderly gentleman in a motorised scooter had decided he'd had enough and was reversing out of my show. I wouldn't have minded, but we suffered two more interruptions while he executed a three-point-turn.

At least we get paid for all this kind of indignation. Danger money, you might call it. That is unless you suffer the deepest shame known to any club singer - being 'paid off'. This means the management hate you so much, they pay you to go away and leave everyone alone. When it happened to me, I thought they liked me so much they were paying me early. Alas, no.

Too posh for audience participation?

If you think your show is too posh for audience participation, take a look at the pros. Look over the show analyses in the appendix, and you'll see everyone does it from Michael Bublé to the late Amy Winehouse.

Not all audiences are the same though. Generally the more sophisticated they are, the less they'll want to be cajoled into participating. Even though you might get them to join in, they'd often really rather not. If you do decide clapping along is appropriate, always wait till the last third or quarter of the song.

Many singers get the audience clapping right at the start and the audience soon get tired and stop, which lowers the energy level. If you get them clapping towards the end of the song, they'll still be clapping when it's finished, and your applause will be stronger as a result. Since we're on the subject, if you start clapping your hands together either side of the microphone, the audience will just hear a dull thud. Either don't let your hands actually touch or better still clap one hand against your forearm, although, you'll find some of the audience will just copy you, silently clapping their hand against their arm!

Audience interaction and the unpredictability that comes with it is part of the appeal of live theatre and something that television and radio are trying to cash in on. "We want to hear your thoughts," they say, constantly nagging us to phone in, email, video-message and press red buttons. Does anybody really care? I'm not so sure. In the theatre you know instantly what your audience thinks, and believe me, getting heckled has much more impact than a belated tweet.

Secret 7: Love Your Musicians

"A gentleman is someone who knows how to play the banjo and doesn't." Mark Twain

As a singer you're completely reliant on the band to make your show work. You'll want to be on good terms from the moment your rehearsal begins so they're on your side and keen to do their best for you. All the band want from you is professionalism. They want you to show up on time, know what you're doing and give them clear music to play.

Musical Director Barry Robinson says what impresses him most is all round professionalism:

> That includes the way you look, the way you conduct yourself and how much you genuinely care about what you do. Remember, you don't get a second chance to make a first impression.

Tim Fulker agrees:

> Be on time, be prepared, be courteous, and above all make sure your arrangements are clean, clear and correct. They should be presented on good quality paper and with properly spaced bars and staves so they are easy to read.

Let's look at how to commission great musical arrangements

and gain the musicians' support during your rehearsals.

First impressions count

Every musical director I've met agrees the best way to make a good first impression with the band is to use high quality musical arrangements. It shows that you take your work seriously.

Before making her name with the UK's big bands, Eleanor Keenan learned her trade the old fashioned way, shlepping around Ireland's dance halls in a tour-van working with different orchestras. Often with little or no rehearsal, she relied on her arrangements to be correct and easy to read. Like Tim, she urges everyone to, "Invest in the best musical arrangements you can afford."

Barry Robinson puts it like this:

> Arrangements are the tools of your trade and, if done properly, will last a lifetime. If a singer turns up with dog-eaten parts, full of scribbles and crossings out, it suggests they don't care. The best arrangements don't have to be overly difficult. They should simply communicate all the information that's needed, but still allow room for the music to breathe.

Fellow musical director Joel Pierson says attention to detail matters:

> Be careful where the page turns and repeat signs appear in arrangements, especially for pianists. Good arrangements are expensive. You get what you pay for, so be weary if they're cheap - they might be good enough to get the job done, but you won't earn any respect from the band.

Find a pianist
The first step to commissioning an arrangement is to find a good pianist. Steve Ross advises anyone to:

> Link up with a pianist who'll work with you to create the arrangements. These days, as singers are bringing to the cabaret stage songs from so many different sources (often far different from the traditional American Songbook) good arrangements are more important than ever. I find it a fascinating challenge to take a rock song and arrange it in a completely new way. When it's done right it can be very effective. Be careful though, a less than compelling lyric might be exposed as such! Ernest is fine, but it might not be entertaining.

Once you've found the ideal collaborator, you'll need to decide on keys, cuts, vamps, play-offs and anything special you want from the band. Remember, it's your show - you can do what you like. Creating arrangements and putting medleys together is a fulfilling and creative process. It's your opportunity to put your own stamp on your music and your show. If you're paying for arrangements you might as well make them different to everyone else's. Take your time to get everything right at this stage, mistakes can be costly to correct.

The different compositions of bands
Another major consideration is which instruments you have your charts written for. I've been commissioning arrangements for over 35 years and now have over 500 for jazz trio up to full orchestra. From my mistakes, I've learned the best way to have them written. It look me years of trial and error to get it right. If you're just starting out, what I'm about to tell you could save

you a lot of time and literally $1000s. Excluding big band and symphony orchestras, here are the most common band sizes you'll be asked to work with::

- **Piano only**
- **Rhythm section only:** piano, bass, drums, guitar (optional).
- **Rhythm plus one horn:** piano, bass, drums, guitar (optional), sax (usually plays tenor, alto, flute and clarinet).
- **Rhythm plus one horn, second keys and percussion:** piano, second keyboard/percussion (a percussionist with congas, timpani, shakers and an electronic keyboard for filling out the sound with string, brass etc.), bass, drums, guitar, sax (usually plays tenor, alto, flute and clarinet).
- **Rhythm plus three horns:** piano, bass, drums, guitar (optional), trumpet, sax (usually plays tenor, alto, flute and clarinet), trombone.
- **Rhythm plus four or five horns:** piano, bass, drums, guitar (optional), trumpet 1, trumpet 2 (optional), alto sax, tenor sax (both saxes usually also play flute and clarinet), trombone.

Your charts need to work with whatever line-up you're likely to face, and that can make things tricky for your arranger.

There are different ways to approach this challenge. Many singers have separate sets of horn parts arranged for each line up. When they have three horns they use one set of parts, when they have four they use another set.

I don't want to carry all that extra music around (my bags already weigh too much as it is) so this is my approach:

- First, I have everything cued on the piano part. If necessary the song will work with just voice and piano.
- My bass and drum parts rarely change, but the guitar is

written as an optional instrument - if it's available I'll use it, but the chart will work either way.
- I have a single horn chart written for when there's just one brass player. Not all brass instruments can read the same piece of music, so my single horn part is written specifically for tenor sax. Don't cut corners by giving the solo sax player your lead trumpet part. She might be able to make it work, but it's not ideal.
- I have parts for a five-piece horn section but the second trumpet and second sax parts are optional. The charts work perfectly well with just one trumpet, one sax and trombone. If I have the other guys I just use the extra charts. The lead sax part is written for alto, the second (optional) sax is tenor.

I know, it gets complicated. I wouldn't necessarily use these 'compromised' charts in a recording session, but for a live cabaret where practicality is a major consideration, they work very well.

A note about instrumental breaks

If people have paid to see you do your thing at a cabaret club or music festival, you can afford to be somewhat indulgent. At private parties, corporate events and on cruise ships, people tend to have shorter attention spans. Having too many instrumental breaks (while you and the audience look on) might be problematic and sadly, they'll get bored.

When you see a production show with a cast of singers and dancers, there's always something to keep the senses stimulated. If there is an instrumental break, the dancers, moving set pieces and clever lighting can keep everyone engaged. You probably don't have such tricks at your disposal, so unless you fancy doing backflips in a skin-tight body stocking, I suggest you keep your instrumental breaks to a minimum.

When the musicians are being featured, be aware of what you're doing on stage. People are still looking at you. Step aside, look at the soloist and be totally engaged. That might sound obvious but it's quite common to see acts who actually look bored while their musicians are playing wonderful solos. They start fiddling with their mic stand or looking over their set list. If you don't care, neither will your audience. Remember, the audience will look where you direct them. They will follow your focus so make sure it's in the right place.

The difficulty level

Levels of musicianship vary. Some venues have terrific players who read well and are used to playing a great show after ninety minutes of rehearsal, but you won't always be so lucky. It's not unusual for the musicians to speak very little English, which can mean that written instructions on the parts might be lost.

When I started singing, my charts were quite straightforward, so just about anyone could play them. As I began to work with more experienced musicians they'd sometimes complain the writing was too simple and a bit boring to play. Keen to keep the band happy, I found another arranger and had my whole show rewritten to give them more of a challenge. The results were mixed.

After performing my Nat Cole tribute show at jazz festivals across the UK, I was asked to take it onto a small cruise ship. What should have been a 90 minute rehearsal turned into three days! I kid you not. The charts were beautifully written, and though my usual musicians ate them up, they were just too much for these poor guys. The result - I never took those charts, or anything like them, on a ship again. It's not that the ship guys were necessarily bad musicians, they just weren't jazz specialists. It was my fault because the charts were inappropriate for that gig.

I've now found a balance of difficulty versus effectiveness with my charts. They are easy enough for any decent musician to play, but present some challenges for better players. The trick is having all the basic information there but leaving space for the more experienced players to add their own touch. As Barry Robinson said, let the charts "breath". This gives them a chance to embellish and improvise. It's a compromise, but why bother making life unnecessarily hard for yourself or the band?

If you find yourself working with musicians who struggle to read your music, singer Tara Khaler says:

> Know which charts are the safest and easiest to play, and avoid giving the tricky ones to less competent musicians. Meet with the musicians a few days before your show and highlight any problematic areas. If necessary, be prepared to change your show to suit the ability of the band.

It's also worth remembering that using songs with lots of tempo changes can be making a rod for your own back. All those changes need directing, and unless you want to conduct the band yourself, you might be better off choosing other material. It's a lot to ask of any musician, who's never seen your charts before, to remember various tempo changes perfectly, after one short rehearsal. Consider practicality as much as creativity with the songs you put into your show.

Stock charts

Unsurprisingly, Joel Pearson thinks it's better to commission your own arrangements, especially if you want your act to be original. "If you find an arrangement 'off-the-shelf'," he warns, "so can everyone else."

Band leader Joey Mix says your arrangements tell the band a

lot about your level of professionalism. He warns:

> Poor charts will make the band angry and frustrated. Though they might not say anything to you, it will affect their mood on stage. Expect to pay anything from $50 for a cheap stock chart that isn't too good, up to around $300-400 for a standard tune arranged professionally just for you.

Despite the dangers though, I think there are times it makes sense to buy stock charts. If, for example, a client requests a special song for a private party that I will probably never use again, I'm not prepared to spend a lot of money. I've also wasted money on arrangements of songs that I thought would suit me really well, only to find they don't suit me at all. Sometimes you only know if something works when you're actually performing it in front of an audience. These days, I will usually start by finding a cheap backing-track online, just to make sure the song is really a good fit for me. If it works, then I might buy a stock chart to try a song out with a band. If that works well, I'll go ahead and commission my own version, confident it will be worth the expense. If you need to save money, ordering stock arrangements can be useful when you're starting out. I've included contact details for a few suppliers and my favourite arrangers at cabaretsecrets.com. Search for "arrangements" to find the article.

Rehearsing with the band

When it comes to rehearsing your show with the band, Joey Mix says:

> Show up early, well ahead of time. If you have specific sound or technical issues that need sorting out, do it

before the band arrives, so they're not sitting around waiting for you to fix issues that have nothing to do with them.

I usually introduce myself to the tech team (sound, lights and Production Manager) the evening before my show. I will make sure they have everything they need and answer any questions. This can make a huge difference to the rehearsal the next day. People like to feel comfortable, prepared and know they are working with a professional.

It sounds obvious, but make sure your music comes with a set list and is already in order, ready to go. I like to place the music on the musicians' stands well before any of them arrive for the rehearsal. Again, it just looks good and creates the right impression.

When you rehearse, should you count the songs off yourself or leave that to the musical director? Joey says:

> Singers often take on more of the conducting role during the show which can be a little frustrating for the MD when he has a tight band that's used to following him.

There are times though when I think it makes sense for the act to take control. If you have a very quick segue and know the tempo well, it can be quicker and easier for everyone if you just count the band off yourself. The MD will either have to reset his metronome, or since time is short and he's under pressure, he might guess the tempo and get it wrong.

I often direct the band at the end of dramatic songs. I am doing this more for the benefit of the audience, than the band. I want it to look like I am in control, but musicians are still watching the MD, who in turn, is watching me.

If you need to say something during a rehearsal, it's usually better to avoid giving comments directly to the individual musicians. Instead, go through the musical director. This is especially important if things are going wrong and there are personality issues within the band. By nature, I am a very calm person, but to my shame, I've lost my cool on more than one occasion with musicians who don't seem to be paying attention or have turned up with an attitude. I should have minded my own business and let the MD deal with it.

I once sat in on a rehearsal for flautist Bettine Clemen. Halfway through her rousing Carmen Medley, the music would stop and everyone had to wait for the pianist to turn the page and start to play the next section. Three times the band stopped and three times the pianist forgot to turn the page and play. Bettine, normally the very model of patience, was growing more intense. "I have explained this to you three times now! Each time you nod and say 'Okay', and then you forget to play. It's not difficult. Just turn the page and play. What's the problem? Can't you understand plain English?" At this point the musical director at the drums interjected, "No," he said, "he does not speak English. He has not understood a single word you've been telling him."

Trust your musical director. He'll know how to get the result you want in the easiest way possible.

It was a source of embarrassment to me for years that I don't read music. I used to bluff my way through rehearsals, hoping no one would catch me out, by throwing in sentences like, "Can you observe the dynamics before the rallentando and push through the triplets at letter D?" I needn't have worried. As Joey says, "It doesn't matter if you don't read music, as long as you can sing."

As you gain more experience, learn the bar numbers or letters at the tricky points of each song. This means that when you rehearse you can tell the band, "The bridge can be a little tricky, so let's rehearse from letter G first, just to get that section right."

Doing that will instantly earn you a few points with the band. You're not bluffing it or showing off, you're just making the rehearsal process as efficient as possible.

Don't rehearse all your patter during a rehearsal, just the cue lines that lead in the next song, so the MD is well used to hearing them. Each time you rehearse a song, always give the cue line. The more the MD hears it the better the chance of him catching it during the show.

Who's in charge?

Normally all the information the MD needs will be on the piano part, but often the MD is not the pianist. This is why you need instructions for the leader on every piece of music. This also means that everyone can see what's going on, even when they're not playing themselves.

For example, let's assume the trumpet player is the MD and during a song she rests for 16 bars during which there's a sax solo and a tempo change. Her part will just show the 16 bar rest. She will have no idea that she needs to direct a new tempo or cue the sax player. To direct the band properly, she'll need to know what everyone is doing, all the time. Ask your arranger to include all the information an MD might need on all the parts.

Musicians changing parts

There are different ways to write charts. What may be ideal for one musician could be confusing to another. There are, for example, different musical conventions in the USA and the UK. It never ceases to amaze me how I can use a chart for years without a comment or complaint, then one day someone will tell me a particular chord is wrong or a whole section impossible to play.

It took me years to realise that often musicians see a mistake and just fix it without mentioning it. Once in a while, someone will make a big fuss about something, but that's all right. Make a note of what's wrong and if necessary have the charts corrected. If you've made a good impression with the musicians and they like you, they'll usually be happy to spend a few minutes fixing any small errors and making it work for you.

Taking care of your musicians' welfare

If your gig is a corporate event or a private party, like a wedding, you will probably be the one responsible for the welfare of the musicians on the day. Please, take this seriously. You should agree the following details with the client, well before the big day, and have every detail agreed clearly in a contract. Having everything in black-and-white is in everyone's interest. It leaves no room for confusion and everyone gets what they need:

- Adequate parking should be provided. Who will pay for parking fees or congestion charges?
- A changing area with mirror, clothes rail, sufficient chairs and tables, power-points and so on.
- Agree clearly what refreshments should be provided and when. Do you require hot food or just sandwiches? Alcohol or not? Drinks on arrival? If you're supposed to be playing after your meal and the meal is late… what happens?
- Exact performance times should be agreed. This is especially important because events often run over and your client needs to be very clear of your finish time. You could even write into your contact the extra fees that would be due in the event of a late finish.

Summary

Your musicians are an integral part of your show. With very little rehearsal it can be a challenge for them to deliver a solid performance, so it's up to you to give them all the support they need.

- Make a good first impression with the band by turning up early to rehearsals.
- Memorise the names of your musicians.
- Always be polite and respectful.
- If you are responsible for the welfare of the musicians, e.g. at a corporate event, make sure they are properly fed, have plenty of refreshments and somewhere comfortable to change and rest. This should all be agreed in advance in the contract.
- If there's a problem, talk to the musical director, not the individual band members.
- Use good, clean, well-written musical arrangements. Be prepared to spend money on your charts, your reputation relies on it.

When you think of the start up costs for most businesses, your initial outlay is small. Good arrangements last a lifetime, and this is your livelihood. Treat your musicians with respect and they'll give you 100%.
.

Secret 8: Make It Look Good and It Will Sound Twice As Good

Nat 'King' Cole said:

> Jazz musicians could learn one thing, and that's presentation. Always think, 'How I am going to present it? Am I going to be lit right?' Make it look good and it will sound twice as good to the average guy because everything with the public is visual. They don't care what problems you've had to figure out or if you've had any rest, they just want to be entertained, and that's where showmanship comes in.

Wise words from one of the most respected singers and jazz pianists of all time. In fact, Cole's lighting had been so atmospheric for one Chicago concert, the reviewer mentioned how much it had dramatically enhanced the whole performance.

From clothes and make-up to lighting and production, here are a few tips on how to look and sound your best on stage.

Lighting

I learned the hard way to keep lighting simple. In one venue I failed to realise that the technician was new, and well, clueless. The only thing he was good at was reassuring me everything would be all right. It was a disaster. Blackouts in the middle of songs, house lights on and off for no reason, and so much haze I almost called Search and Rescue. During one ballad the 'intimate look' around the piano was suddenly replaced with every light flashing at full speed. It looked like a school disco. When it's done right though, lighting can take your show to the next level.

I've seen Tony Bennett and his quartet twice at London's Royal Albert Hall. On both occasions I was fascinated by the lighting design. Changing the mood with the music, focussing our eyes on the soloists, and occasionally bringing the lights up in the house to build the audience's reaction. Most people wouldn't have even noticed what the lights were doing, only the effect they were having. Many venues these days have amazing lights at their disposal, creating effects and shapes (with gobos) on stage. The lights for Bennett's show were old-school, simple and effective. It showed me that you don't necessarily need all the latest gear to light a show well. Basic equipment in the right hands is usually enough. Like the musical arrangements, the things Bennett chatted about and the songs he performed, the lighting was an integral part of the show's success.

The Royal Albert Hall seats over 4000 people, but even if you're performing in a tiny cabaret room with very little equipment, you should liaise with the technical staff to discuss the kind of moods you want to create during your show.

Working with a lighting engineer

Many lighting technicians I meet are in their 20s and not familiar with the songs I like to sing. I've learned not to make assumptions and to give them good information to work with. That said, information overload can be a problem. All they really need to understand are the moods you're trying to create and how each song ends.

Belgium born lighting designer, Tom Derycke was attracted to cruise ships because of the state-of-the-art equipment onboard. He'd lit many arena size shows with the same amount of equipment available in a nine hundred seat theatre at sea. With over two hundred automated lights at his disposal, almost anything's possible. As he told me, he doesn't need that much information from the singer:

> Obviously you need to know the set list, when the act will talk and when she'll segue straight to the next song. It's most important to know how each song is going to end - in a big way or intimately - because that's where I can add some nice effects. Overall, it's best to keep things simple.

Don't bother trying to impress the engineer with technical jargon, just tell them in everyday language if the song is fast, slow, happy, sad, whether there's a band feature, a drum solo and how it ends. You might ask for a "snap" ending, where a lighting effect happens right on the last beat, or a "slow fade out" as the last notes of a ballad die away.

"If there are more lighting cues than just 'on' and 'off'," says Steve Ross, "you bet I get involved. I always give the lighting technician a set list with the following short-hand designations I've developed over the years:

- "4" Very bright stage. Reserved for the last number.
- "3" Reds and Special Lavender (the singer's friend). Used most of the time in the act, especially for the patter and the up/rhythm tunes.
- "2" Blues and violets for ballads.
- "1" The Judy Garland - just the spotlight or 'special' on my face. Only to be used once or twice in any show and reserved for the heart-rending ballad moments.

"I also tell them where I want blackouts (mainly right after comedy numbers) and fade-outs (at the end of ballads)."

What makes Steve's system so effective is its simplicity. It's straightforward enough for the most basic lighting rig and the instructions could not be clearer. There's a lot to be said for using the same basic information in larger venues with a more substantial rig. Simple instructions mean you'll never overwhelm an inexperienced engineer, but if you're lucky enough to have someone with time and talent, they'll have lots of freedom to create a bit of magic.

Another New Yorker, Jeff Harnar, says he's learned to trust the experience of the staff on hand so he can concentrate on the show:

> I don't let my energies get too diverted to sound and light concerns," he told me. "If my cue sheets are clear, if I can hear what I need in the monitors, if the musicians have what they need, and I've wandered out into the house during the rehearsal to hear what the audience is getting, and am satisfied, I surrender to their care.
>
> Whether working on land or at sea, I give the lighting tech a running order and cue sheet, showing clearly which songs are up tempo and which are ballads. I also give them a sense of bright or dim and note where I want a 'black-out on button', a 'fade to black' or no black-out at all. I also mark where I think a lighting 'special' might be useful for a specific moment in the set.

Like Steve, Jeff keeps things simple:

> If I'm settling into a run of a show, then it's worth the time to get more actively involved with the lights and sound. The best case scenario for me is to have a

director who is out front as my 'third eye'. One great piece of advice I've gotten is to establish five or six 'looks' with the lighting designer. Then as you tech the show, just call out which 'look' you would like for that song. It's pretty foolproof.

Michael Feinstein now tours with a full-time road manager who takes care of lights and sound. Before that, things were a little different:

> When I first started working, I was ill prepared for such things. I slowly figured it out as I went along. I used to set a few basic lighting moods with the light tech and then discuss where each one could be best used in the show. In the end though, it all depended on my instincts. I had to understand what was possible and quickly assess their ability to execute my vision accurately.
>
> The other thing I would sometimes do is actually request a certain lighting effect from the stage during the show, and then, if it didn't work out properly, I could make a joke about it, letting the audience in on the situation.

That reminds me of a bit of business I saw in Vegas, when an act called out from the stage to the lighting tech, "Can you give me some lighting that will really enhance the next part of my show?" To which the tech made the stage completely black.

It's important you 'block' your show during the rehearsal. This means that while you're singing through your show, you go to the same part of the stage each time, just as you will during the actual performance. This might inspire the engineer to place specials at the piano, or down stage. If he programs this and you change your blocking during the show, the lights won't make any sense.

Good lighting won't always transfer from one theatre to another. Trust your engineer and be open to his suggestions. He will know his rig and what it's capable of better than you.

Remember, you'll often be asking the engineer to design and program your whole show in about 90 minutes. You can't expect too much detail.

Just in case the engineer might have time to start programming my show before the rehearsal starts, I give him a plan identifying each part of the stage with its own number. This means he can tell exactly where I'll be performing at all times (my blocking) and can start programming the lights accordingly.

My lighting directions

To give you an idea of what I do, here's the information I gave to the lighting engineer for part of my show in Brazil:

Coffee Song/Brazil
Area 2. Bright and lively.
Light area 6 as Gary walks down stage for "Brazil".
On last beat, snap to black then fade area 5 to medium look.

Can't Take My Eyes
Area 5. Medium look. No movement.
House lights up a bit when Gary leaves the stage.
At the end, fade to chat light.

Ipanema
Stay on chat light till Gary starts to sing.
Slow fade to area 3. Nothing too intense. Warm colours.
For sax solo: light special on sax player and take spot off Gary.
Fade to black.

Samba Medley
Area 4: Fade in over band vamp. Nice colours, nothing too intense. Use spot to cut through gobos. Gary chats.
When Gary starts to sing, slowly fade some lights out so it's a little more focussed around the stool.
For the second song "One Note Samba" (in English) brighten a bit.
For the brass break, brighten the horns and area 6.
Snap to black at end.
Chat light.

Mas Que Nada
Stay on chat light till band starts.
Area 6. Bright, fun, colourful.
Spot musicians for their solos.
Snap to black

Gipsy Kings Medley + play-off
Area 6. Bright, fun, colourful.
House lights up a little when Gary leaves the stage.
There are 6 songs in this medley, make a small change for each one: Bamboleo, Volare, Bem Bem Maria, Djobi Djoba, Baila Me, Bamboleo (reprise).
Snap to black at end.
Restore lights for play-off and bows.

Sound

I asked Jazz Mouse studio's Paul Fawcus how a singer, with little technical knowledge of sound, can get the best result from the technician they're working with. "Communication, communication, communication!" he said.

> Ignorance on both sides has created a culture of mistrust but a little effort all round speaks volumes. It should be a bi-directional exchange and contrary to

popular belief, neither party is telepathic! It's a common misconception that all technicians are sound engineers. Most venues' staff are expected to cover all disciplines to a 'working' level, so ask what experience the technician has. Talk to one another but more importantly learn to communicate in a common language. At a rudimentary level, sound can be divided into top, middle and bottom and I often think it helps to think of sound as light, for example, 'too bright', 'too dark' and so on. Using simple terms like these is more helpful than, 'It's rubbish, I don't like it!'

The obvious way to promote good communication is to introduce yourself to the sound engineer before the rehearsal starts. Tell him how you like to sound through the PA, what you want through the monitors and so on.

Use a rider
Being prepared in advance of the rehearsal and letting the sound technician know any special requirements can save headaches later on. One of my favourite engineers, Kay Richardson, told me:

My main issue with singers is the lack of a proper technical rider. I need to know exactly what equipment they'll need for their show in advance. Sometimes they turn up for the rehearsal and ask for click-tracks or in-ear monitors for a whole group. That takes time to set up which means the whole band and crew can be waiting for thirty minutes. I also get frustrated with poor microphone technique.

Microphones
I have my preferences, but I'm usually happy to use whatever

microphone the venue gives me. I realise that may sound like I should care more, but in my experience a basic SM58 can sound great with a good engineer and singer. There are better mics for my voice, but I think we have got other things to worry about. That said, if you have found a mic you love, consider touring with it. Take professional advice to find one that's best suited to your voice. Paul Fawcus says:

> When you get the chance, experiment with different microphones so you have some knowledge of what they can do. You'll find that the sound can change dramatically depending on how close it is to your mouth. Think of it as a torch - if it's not shining at your face the engineer can't do much to help you. The same applies to monitors. If it's pointing at your knees or shooting over your head it won't be very effective. A well placed piece of wood to alter the angle is generally all that's needed.

Rehearsing for sound

Once the rehearsal starts, give the engineer enough time to work on the sound before you start commenting and refining. I usually wait until I've sung three songs before I start asking for changes.

"When rehearsing," says engineer Chris Peters, "you should at least top and tail some of the songs to give the sound engineer a good idea of your dynamic range. Try to be consistent - sing at the same levels in the rehearsal as you will during the performance."

Sound changes significantly once an audience is seated. People and fabric absorb the sound, making it warmer and the room less 'lively'. Bear this in mind and trust your engineer to make the necessary adjustments for showtime.

Never be intimidated to approach the engineer. If you're not sure about something, don't be afraid to ask. Chris likes it when an artiste takes an active interest in the sound. "Walk around the house so you can listen to the overall mix. If nothing else the engineer will know you're serious about getting the sound right."

Paul Fawcus agrees. "Don't become fixed around the monitors - move around the stage and the house to see how the sound changes."

Avoiding tension

Percussionist Kuba Kawnik tries not to be fussy about his sound. He thinks the audience doesn't care much about the general mix - only if it's too loud. He's mindful that he's a guest in the engineer's domain and demanding too many changes might create tension. "Sometimes," he explains, "when you let a small issue go and give the sound engineer some space, he may be more willing to help you. Pushing too hard can have the opposite effect." His tip is to go to the theatre and listen to other shows:

> If you notice the engineer consistently mixes the bass too quiet or the trumpet too loud or you don't like the overall mix, you can diplomatically mention this to the engineer before you even start your rehearsal, nipping any issues in the bud. Diplomacy is the key.

Use plain language

You don't need to know technical language to explain what you need to the engineer. As Kay Richardson told me, sometimes the look on the artiste's face can be enough:

> Almost every singer I work with speaks in basic layman's terms, so now I get it. I even find I can tell if

they are happy by watching their reactions - if they make a weird face, I know I need to make more adjustments! At the end of the day, as long as the singer's happy, I am too.

Production

Many venues, especially cruise ships, offer incredible technical opportunities for artistes to enhance their shows, but be careful, the more technical elements you have in your show, the more that can go wrong. I once saw a violinist playing a beautiful classical piece when, for no apparent reason, the production manager lowered the projection screen. We all watched in horror as it slowly descended right in front of her. Noticing, just in time, she managed to deftly limbo under the screen without missing a note.

Aside from lighting effects, here are some of the things that may be at your disposal.

Risers. These are sections of the stage that can be moved up or down on cue. You can place each part of the band on their own riser and set them to different heights to add more interest to the stage. You can use them yourself to sing from different parts of the stage. You could, for example, open your show on a high riser, which slowly lowers to stage level during the song. There may also be a pit riser. This is large section at the front of the stage that lowers right down into the musician's pit. It's sometimes used in production shows to bring performers on or off stage through the floor.

Scrim. A scrim is a large piece of loosely woven material that usually fills the width of the stage. If lighting is thrown on the front of a scrim drop, with no lighting behind, it becomes opaque. If lighting on the front is reduced and the scrim is lit from behind, it becomes transparent, revealing what's behind. I sometimes use this effect to open my show. I start the first song on a high riser and just have my face lit through the scrim. Lifting the scrim part way through the song to reveal the band adds impact.

Mid-stage curtains. Many theatres have a selection of curtains or drops available for use. You could, for example, sing a ballad with a mid-stage curtain down to hide the band and keep all the focus on you.

Live video. Having your show filmed and projected live onto screens during your show (known as IMAG for Image Magnification) can be very effective. Some theatres I've worked can show the images on large video walls at the back of the stage. Pianists and magicians will often use IMAG so the audience can see all the action, close up.

Projection. Many acts will turn up with video footage on memory sticks to be projected onto side screens as a pre-show or during their performance. If this is an important part of your show, consider using a programme like QLab which can automate pretty much everything, leaving little to chance.

If all this sounds a bit daunting don't be afraid to ask for help. Production Manager, Vasil Hristov, likes it when an act seeks his advice:

> We know our theatre very well. We've been doing different shows in there everyday for years. That's literally thousands of shows! We care about what we do and enjoy the challenge of helping a new act stage their show. Almost anything's possible and it's an

opportunity for us to step up and do something different. At the end of the day we'll do everything we can to help every artiste look and sound their best.

What to wear

Listen, I'm no stylist, but I've seen enough ill dressed performers to learn a thing or two about what to wear on stage.

If you're in the UK, you'll already know that High Street favourite Marks & Spencer is good for three things: food, underwear and the 'Active Waistband'. This clever innovation discreetly introduced a large piece of elastic into the waistband of a pair of trousers. Now anyone with delusions of weight-loss can confidently buy trousers two sizes smaller than they ought. Instead of having to undo their pants after dinner, the Active Waistband takes the strain. In fact, no matter how active their waist gets, these minor miracles never let them down. That's great for the real world, but when you're on stage, style comes before comfort.

Marlene Dietrich had her priorities right. Still performing well into her 70s, she had her hair tightly braided before donning a wig, the stage strategically darkened to camouflage her age and she wore a special all-over rubber girdle to maintain her hourglass figure. Apparently, the ironclad garment was so restrictive to her movement that at one performance in Washington, she fell into the orchestra pit and broke her hip. At least she looked good on the way down.

Tailor made or off-the-peg?

Think about having your clothes custom made. It's less expensive than you might think. If you're lucky enough visit to Asia, a handmade suit can cost less than $100. A few years ago I met Danny Kon, Director at Hong Kong's 'Cosmo Circle Custom Tailor'. He's been making my suits ever since. These days I catch him on one of his annual 'fitting tours' in London. Danny told me:

> When it comes to clothing even a luxury fashion house can't provide a suit as unique as one custom made by a skilled tailor. This alone is reason enough for a singer, whose artistry is expressing their individuality, to get a tailored suit.
>
> Make sure the tailor you choose is reputable and understands what you're looking for. Style wise, a two buttoned, notch lapel suit with side vents can work with any body shape, but first and foremost is the fit. Once you've had a precise fitting, we use a fitting mould to maintain consistency. This is a dummy made according to each client's unique measurements. It means you can be sure of a perfect fit without having to see us in person every time. Perfect for anyone ordering from overseas.
>
> If you don't have a figure like a model's, wearing a good suit can still make you the sharpest man in the room.

Much of this applies to clothes for women too. For me, I like to use a lightweight fabric, so I don't get too hot; a mix of wool and manmade fibres to reduce creasing; and I have my jacket sleeves flared at the ends so the cuffs of my shirt don't get caught outside the jacket during a show.

Even if you're buying 'off-the-peg', a local seamstress can make adjustments. You don't have to spend a lot of money. A few tweaks can turn an everyday High Street suit into something special.

Think of what you wear on stage as a costume. It's your work-wear. Wear it for the show and maybe a signing or 'meet and greet' afterwards, but that's it. Never go to the bar or a restaurant after your show without changing.

Where possible, have your clothes professionally pressed before each performance. If necessary, travel with a steamer and use it, even between sets.

You probably don't have dancing fountains or the Rockettes on hand helping to distract the audience when you're performing. It's just you, and looking good is your responsibility. Even if you forgo a rubber girdle, what you wear should be the envy of everyone in the room.

Make-up

When I first started performing, I didn't know my powder puff from my blush brush. Where I come from, it takes a strong man to admit to wearing eyeliner. I thought make-up was for girls. I certainly had no idea how to apply foundation and when the time came, I worked on the premise: the more the better. I remember sweating so much during one community theatre performance, the tonne of foundation I'd applied was running down my face like paint down a fence. Half way through my 'Frank Valli Medley' it got into my eyes. Temporarily blinded, I had to sing the whole of 'Walk Like A Man' through a glaze of Avon Cashmere Kiss.

I asked M.A.C Pro Senior Make-up Artist, Dean Rudd, what advice he could have offered to save my peach blushes back then:

> It's important to select make-up that has a good coverage but is also kind to the skin. Often products can be layered or grouped to achieve a better effect. There have been many breakthroughs with technology and cosmetics. Long-wear foundations, for example, have good staying power, even under hot lights. They feel comfortable and look realistic.

Powder foundations are great for theatre work as they have a matte finish, good coverage and help to keep sweat and moisture at bay.

When defining your features such as eyes, pick a pencil or eye shadow that has good pigmentation (colour) and a matte finish. A selection of brown tones in various shades will allow you to define and make-up, not just the eye area, but also the brows. Lashes should always be defined using a good waterproof mascara.

Lip pencils are a good way of adding colour and definition to the lips. Lip pencils tend to stay in place a lot better than lipsticks and they allow you to draw or alter your lip shape.

A shot of warmth and colour is often needed on the face to complete the look. Powder blush in rosy and peach shades are perfect for adding natural warmth and radiance to the skin. Matte bronzing powders are a good way to add a subtle tanned look to your make-up.

Always assess your own features to determine the nature and strength of the make-up you need to apply. For example, small eyes can be made to look bigger with clever application of make-up: liner can be placed slightly lower than the bottom lash line to create the illusion that the eyes are larger. The same principle can be applied to the socket line of the eye. Cotton wool buds can be used to soften eye pencils which will create a less harsh look, especially for male performers.

That's all great advice, but if you're not used to applying make-up, you may just want the quickest and easiest way to look normal under the glare of stage lighting.

I asked Sarah Maxwell - an LA based make-up artist whose

client list includes Vogue, the X-Factor and Robert Redford - if she had any tips for blokes like me:

> Moisturising the face is an important first step before applying make-up. Get the right sponges and brushes, and make sure all your facial hair is properly groomed and quaffed. Use sweat-proof (alcohol based) and waterproof products, (like water proof mascara) to help your make-up last through your performance.

Personally, I only use M.A.C. cosmetics. For stage work I apply a light base covering of moisturising foundation with my fingers, then use a pad to add bronzing powder to my cheeks and forehead. I quickly dust my face with a transparent fixing powder, add a bit of definition to my eyebrows with a brown pencil and use a bit of eyeliner on my lower lids. That's it. I know I'd look better if I took more time, but for me, it's enough.

I asked Sarah to explain the main differences between make-up for photo shoots and the stage:

> I would say heaviness of the application, though there are exceptions to the rules. Normally, make-up for the stage needs to be seen under harsh stage lights. Photo shoot make-up is usually lit more subtly.
>
> The other main difference is in the blending. For theatre, the make-up is more carved out and visible to create the character. In photo shoot make-up, the key to a flawless application is blending all visible lines so the application looks seamless.
>
> My advice when using stage make-up is to create layers for yourself, so it lasts, and to seal your creation with a fixer like Kryolan Fixing Spray.

Summary

It's not enough for your show to sound great - it has to look great too. Until you feel comfortable, my advice is to K.I.S.S: Keep It Simple, Stupid.

- Make sure your stage outfits fit perfectly and look great.
- Buy a steamer and use it.
- Get professional advice on what stage make-up is right for you.
- Everyone needs some make-up to counter the bright stage lights.
- Give the lighting tech enough information without overwhelming them.
- Take the time to introduce yourself to the sound tech before your rehearsal starts and give them time to work before you start asking for changes.
- For production, less is more. Too much can be distracting and even reduce the impact of your performance.
- Don't be afraid to ask for help.
- Time is always at a premium. I usually struggle to rehearse the band and review the lights in two hours. Each additional technical element you introduce to your show will add more rehearsal time. An extended rehearsal won't win you any friends in the production team, so if you're making everyone work extra hard for you, it had better be worth it.

If you're just starting, keep your show simple and straightforward. Why overwhelm yourself? Ask the venue's production manager for their advice. If you have spare rehearsal time, use it to review and improve your lighting. Only when your basic show is rock solid should you begin introduce new technical elements.

Secret 9: Record a CD

Mark Shenton thinks it's a great idea to "Get a CD together. There's nothing like having a CD as a shop window, both to attract bookings and also give audiences something they can buy to take away with them."

Like many cabaret singers, Sinead Blanchard found that when someone's enjoyed a show, they want to take away a souvenir. "People were asking me for CDs all the time," she told me, "and that gave me the impetus to finally record something. Everyone who enjoyed the show wanted a recording of just that, the actual show. So, for me, the song list was easy."

The other benefits of recording the songs you perform all the time is that you already know them well and you have the musical arrangements. This means you'll know exactly how the album will sound and you won't need much rehearsal time. In the studio, time is money. These days a recording contract is hard to come by, so the chances are you'll be self-funding your albums and that can be expensive.

The recording process

Paul Fawcus says shared some great advice for anyone ready to go into the recording studio:

> The more preparation you can do before you start the first day's recording, the better the results will be. Learn the material; there's nothing worse than hearing, 'I'm not sure how this bit goes...' it's your time you're wasting. Find examples of the kind of music you want

to make so everyone's singing from the same hymn-sheet from day one.

Print or write out very clear parts: ten staves per page and four bars per stave, and bring a copy for the producer/engineer to enable edits and drop ins. If possible, create click-tracks (the studio can easily do this for you).

If you're recording to pre-recorded backing tracks, liaise with the studio before you buy them. They'll want to know what format they're in, the bit-rate and sample rate. I'd always advocate sending them in advance of the recording day and always keep a backup copy to hand.

Finally, rest well before the sessions and drink plenty of water. Dress for comfort; it's going to be a long day.

Take your time

My advice is to take your time. Once your CD's released there's no going back. Paul speaks from experience when he says:

> If you've written six songs pick the best three. Don't try to record all six in one go. You're better off recording three tracks every three months and taking your time, rather than trying to do everything in one day. You'll still have to allow time for edits, overdubs and mixing.

It can cost thousands and take months, maybe years, planning the songs, the arrangements, finding the right producer, the studio, the musicians. At the end you proudly show your beautifully packaged masterpiece to your friends and family... they shower you with praise... you get a few thousand copies pressed and they go on sale. But wait. Let a few months pass and give that CD another listen. With fresh ears and a new perspective, you'll probably be surprised just how much you wish you could go back and change.

I've recorded a lot of albums and it was only by the ninth that I finally realised that on review, they always seemed to follow a rule of thirds. One third of the tracks still stood up to scrutiny, I could listen and still feel proud of my work; one third I could take or leave; and the rest... what was I thinking?

To try and break this predictable pattern, when I recorded my last album at Abbey Road, I resisted the temptation to release it straightaway. I put it to one side and tried to forget about it. Six months later, with fresh ears, I gave it another listen. Sure enough, four of the tracks were below par. There was dodgy intonation, poorly executed phrases, and in one case I even sang the wrong lyrics. Even with a good team around me, none of us spotted these mistakes in the studio. Thankfully I had the chance to fix them. When the album was finally released I knew it would have longevity and I could listen to it without feeling the pinch of regret - well worth the wait and the extra studio time.

Cover design

There are plenty of software packages out there for designing your own artwork but unless you really know what you're doing, it's probably better to get professional help.

Sinead Blanchard told me:

> I used a graphic designer who did a great job. I gave him a very clear idea of my target audience, the style I was looking for and how I wanted the final design to represent me as an artiste.
>
> I think that's the best approach. You want your CD to look as professional as anything else out there and, with the right designer, it will.

Packaging

The most popular way to package CDs is the plastic jewel case, but as Fairview Duplication's Jackie Herd points out, there are alternatives:

> Jewel cases are fine if they are being handed out at gigs, but they are easily broken in the post. If you're regularly sending CDs through the mail consider card wallets, Digifiles or Digipaks.

Digipaks are folded cards with a plastic tray insert for the CD, but my preference is the Digifile which is just card, with a slot inside for the disc. Digifiles are light, which means they are cheaper to post; half the width of a jewel case so you'll have space for twice as many and, since they're cardboard, they don't shatter, which is important when travelling.

Find a good studio

As well as choosing the right songs and booking the band, you'll have to consider technical things like Mastering and ISRC codes (see the glossary for more information). My advice is to find a well-established, professional company. Paul Fawcus agrees and thinks it's good to be honest when contacting potential studios:

> Spend time talking to studios and engineers. Be honest about budgetary restrictions and be realistic about what you want to achieve versus what you can achieve - if it's your first project it's unlikely that you can afford forty plus string players!
>
> If you have musician friends that are happy to play for you, don't abuse them! It's a really easy way to lose friends. Once you find an engineer/producer you can trust, do just that - trust them! It's likely they've made a few more records than you. This is different to having

a friend who, 'once saw Madonna live' or who has, 'been to all my gigs and knows how I sound'. Technical knowledge about the voice, how to record it and how to make a record is very important.

As Jackie Herd says, "Although it may cost a bit more to use a reputable firm, you're more likely to end up with a better product. It'll be worth it in the long run."

The end of the CD?

All of this is becoming a moot point as fewer people own CD players and buy CDs. Acts are now experimenting with download cards or selling their music on USB memory sticks. So far, most people will still buy something after a show because they want a keepsake of their experience. Thank goodness they do because the money we earn from streaming services like Spotify is a joke. The old model of selling CDs to pay for your album is dying and acts need to find new ways to fund their albums. I've paid for two albums now through money raised by crowdfunding. I highly recommend it. The first was for a Christmas album called Big Band Wonderland. The goal was to raise £15,000 in two weeks. We raised over £12,000 in the first day and ended up with £17,859. I'd love to tell you it's because I'm blessed with irresistible powers of persuasion but like everything else, it came down to hard work. Yes, I am lucky enough to have a loyal following, but I knew I couldn't just rely on that. I planned a whole marketing campaign and started priming my fans weeks before the appeal was launched. Everything was planned ahead of time, even all the social media posts. I had two well-known guest-singers on the album to give it a wider appeal. I was creative with the rewards for fans who contributed, even getting people I knew to contribute by giving away their products. My advice is to truly nurture your fan base.

Maintain a connection with them throughout your career and they are more likely to be there to support you when you need help.

Summary

Producing your own album is major project. Even with time, money and talent there's so much that can go wrong. Even so, says Sinead, it's worth the effort, "It was a steep learning curve but despite the hard graft and trials, it's been incredibly rewarding. How exciting to have your own CD in your hand that you have created from start to finish. And let's not forget that it is you and you alone who will reap the reward from it too!"

Secret 10: Listen To Advice, But Be Careful How You Give It

As you build your show and your career takes off, you'll find advice coming at you from all sides. Everyone will have an opinion on how to do your hair, what songs to sing, what shoes to wear, what to say, what to leave out and so on. Marta Sanders says simply, "Listen to the professionals." Ask the people you admire most for advice. They don't have to be famous provided they're respected for their work. I've seen acts completely unaware that something in their show isn't working. Maybe they're singing the wrong words, their suit is ill-fitting, or they don't wear enough make-up so they look washed out under the lights. Whatever it is, they need to know about it. I'd certainly want to, if it was me.

Let's be honest, giving and receiving criticism can be tricky for all of us. We're not machines. We live for performing and put ourselves on the line every time we stand on stage in front of hundreds or thousands of people. It's only natural to prefer praise and reassurance to criticism.

Michael Feinstein told me:

> I never give a performer notes unless I know them well enough to be certain they truly want them. Even people who claim to want notes sometimes don't really want to hear criticism. Judy Garland always said that after a show, the only thing she wanted to hear was that she was, "F#@king great!" and that's a direct quote. So, if

you do give notes, always wait until the right time to do so. Most important is to consider the motive for giving notes and to be very sensitive to the ego of a performer.

Many artistes I meet are either too sure of themselves to care what anyone thinks, or too insecure to want to know. Sadly, they carry on making the same mistakes over again and miss valuable opportunities to improve. We owe it to ourselves not to fall into that trap.

Never offer criticism unless it is invited.

Be open to criticism

We have to take the initiative. Invite colleagues you respect to give you notes after your shows. I do this as often as I can. While they are usually flattered to be asked, I benefit from free professional input. I don't have to act on everything they say, but it never hurts to listen.

If you've been asked to give notes to a fellow performer, be sensitive. It's not good enough to say you didn't enjoy the show, you need to be very specific. And whatever they tell you, don't give them criticism as soon as they walk off stage, save it for later. Arrange to meet for a coffee the say after the show when everyone has a better perspective.

For a great example of how not to give notes, let me share with you what happened to me just before my second night in a long West End run. I hadn't seen the Musical Supervisor since the opening night. I was anxious to know what he thought, but just assumed no news was good news. Literally, five minutes before showtime, as I was about to go on-stage, he knocked at my door.

"About your show last night," he said.

"Oh yes," I replied, hoping and expecting to hear a few words of encouragement.

"I was very disappointed." My heart sank.

"Oh. Really?"

"Yes. I just didn't really enjoy your performance."

I tried to hide my disappointment and embrace what he had to say; after all, he was there to help. "Okay, so what would you like me to think about for this show? Anything specific?"

"No. It's not really anything specific. It's just a general note. I was disappointed, that's all. Anyway, have a good show." And with that, he left.

I was crushed. What was I supposed to do with that, minutes before my second performance? At least he could have been diplomatic. It turned out he had a reputation for doing this to other performers. I suppose it made him feel important.

The most excruciating example of a tactful cop-out I know came from a comedian friend of mine. Thrilled to find Vic Damone was in the house for one of his shows, he went the extra mile and gave a really great performance. The audience loved it and my pal was thrilled when Vic paid him the honour of coming back stage after the show. What a career highlight to be praised by such a legend. Maybe later they'd become friends, drinking buddies or even work together. Vic introduced himself, then stood and stared at the expectant comedian. Seconds felt like minutes. Eventually Vic spoke, "Nice shoes..." he said, and left.

Instrumentalist Kuba Kawnik loves meeting guests after his show and is always open to their suggestions. He told me:

> We don't play for ourselves, we play for our audience, and sometimes they have good advice. I don't always have to take it, but it's always good to hear. I want to know what the audience likes so I can tweak my show to suit them. For example, if they ask for more classical tunes, I'm happy to oblige. Why not?

That's the kind of open attitude that bookers are looking for, especially on cruise ships, but be warned, there are times when well meaning individuals will tell you exactly what they think about your show, whether you like it or not. Even Mozart wasn't immune. After listening to 'The Abduction from the Seraglio' in 1782, Emperor Joseph II famously told him, "Too many notes, my dear Mozart."

Kuba's right, sometimes people do have interesting suggestions - but be discerning, especially if you're going to take advice from the Emperor of Austria.

Secret 11: Talent Is Only The Starting Point

After I'd been performing in Working Men's Clubs for a year, I took my show to a swanky London cabaret club filled with as many bookers and reviewers as I could persuade to come along. Afterwards, the late Peter Hepple of The Stage wrote something I've never forgotten, "Gary Williams is a fine singer and a welcome addition to London's cabaret scene. Now the real work begins."

I thought I'd made it, but he knew it was just the beginning.

"Talent is only the starting point" Irving Berlin

Ten years later I was invited back to the same room. I declined. I didn't feel ready. All I'd learned in ten years was how little I actually knew. It took another two more years of hard work to feel I finally had a show worthy of a West End cabaret venue.

Singer Tara Khaler has some great advice for new acts, "Don't pretend you know it all already. Expect to learn from your mistakes and be happy to make changes."

No matter how good your act might be, there's always more to learn.

Booking agent Gary Parkes and cruise director Keith Maynard say versatility is one of the keys to being a successful act. As Keith says, "Look at the demographic and nationalities of the audience. Be prepared to make changes to your act depending on who's watching."

If you are working on land you'll also need to develop a fan base. There's little point in having a killer show if no one ever sees it.

Let's look at some of the ways you can refine your act and find an audience to appreciate it.

Using foreign languages in your show

I was always hopeless at languages. After three years of Spanish all I could remember was "la caravana". That means "the caravan". Imagine how I felt when my agent told me his most popular acts were those who could speak Spanish. It was a lot of work for me, but eventually I learned enough Spanish phrases and songs to get the work. Then I had my whole show translated into Portuguese, which instantly made me the obvious choice for two seasons in Brazil. You have no idea how much effort it took, but in the end it was worth it.

To listen to me speak in my show you'd think I was fluent, but off stage, I'm still pretty hopeless. So hopeless in fact, that when people talk to me I go mainly by tone of voice and hand gestures. I'm like a dog.

If someone approaches me after my show and says (in Portuguese): "Thank you for a great show, I have all of Frank Sinatra's original CDs, my wife used to love buying them for me."

I hear: "THANK YOU blah blah blah SHOW blah blah blah blah FRANK SINATRA blah CDs blah blah blah blah LOVE blah BUY blah blah blah."

To which I reply, "Thank you, my CDs are $20 each."

If they say: "You know, my daughter also sings. She's only seven years old but she's very talented. She's even recorded a CD. I wish we had a copy here, I am sure you would love it."

I hear: "Blah blah blah SINGS. Blah blah blah blah blah blah

blah VERY TALENTED. Blah blah blah blah CD. Blah blah blah blah blah blah blah, I blah blah blah WOULD LOVE IT."

To which I reply, "Thank you, my CDs are $20 each."

My language troubles aren't just limited to Brazil. On a recent tour in Japan I signed a CD for a man: "What's your name?" "Somethin," "Yes, but what?" "My name is Somethin," "Yes, I realise it's something but can you be more specific, there's a queue." He had to write it down in the end. As it happened, his name was Somethin. Which reminds me of the time after a concert in Glasgow when I signed my Christmas CD to a Mr Sleigh. His wife nodded and said his first name was Bob. "His parents," she said, "had a sense of humour".

One of Production Manager Vasil Hristov's biggest complaints is acts who don't research their audience:

> If the ship's coming out of Hamburg it's likely there'll be a lot of German speakers on board and the act should be prepared for that. They need to say at least a few words in German and maybe sing a song or two in their language. This is why artistes need a lot of spare material. Even though we usually only require one 50 minute show, they should have a lot of alternatives available so they can appeal to everyone onboard: German, Spanish, Italian, American, British and so on.

Cruise Director, João Wolf told me:

> The challenge for us is finding artistes who can communicate with all of the various ages and nationalities on board. They should know, in advance of their show, who they'll be performing to. For example, in Europe we might have a third Spanish, a third English and a third German or Italian speaking

guests. You, the artiste, need to show you care by at least saying a few words in each language. It's not just a matter of translating everything you say in your show into two or three different languages, you need to rethink the whole approach.

Very few people have the creativity and the will to get this right, but more and more the company is trying to book entertainers who can connect to a wider variety of people.

No one expects you to be able to speak six languages fluently. As João suggests, just saying "Hello," and welcoming international audiences in their language is usually enough. If you're already working on a cruise ship, you'll be surrounded by people from every corner of the globe. Take advantage; ask for help and learn a few easy phrases.

Hector Ruiz is a world-class magician and one of my favourite acts. Spanish by birth, he is also fluent in Portuguese and English. When he needs to use all three languages in his show, he doesn't just translate everything three times. After doing the full set-up in the dominant language, he quickly gives a summary in the other two. He manages to keep the pace of the show (even the comedy) without every leaving anyone behind. It's a great skill.

Later, in secret number 13, I discuss the importance of finding your Unique Sales Point. Something that sets you apart from the thousands of other singers trying to find work. Learning to speak to international audiences is a great USP. If you want to travel and work internationally, stop learning songs and start learning languages.

If you already speak a second or third language, my advice is to use it with caution. Whenever you're talking in German, anyone who doesn't speak German will feel alienated. Go back to English and all the non-English speakers will soon feel bored. Entertaining a multinational audience is a tricky balancing act. You will have to make compromises. If you translate everything you say from English to Spanish to German, your patter will take too long.

When I have a lot of Brazilians in the audience I'll speak to them directly for one whole section, then just give a summary in English. For the next section, I'll address the English speakers first and summarise in Portuguese. This way no one's ignored for too long and the chat stays pretty tight. I never bother trying to tell a joke in one language and then translate it into another. When you've got to the punch line for the second or third time, the moment's gone.

Take the time to learn part of your act in a foreign language, and you'll instantly be in greater demand.

Ask Yourself "Why?"

Everything you add to your show, every little thing, should be carefully considered and be there for a reason. João Wolf says, "You should be asking yourself 'why' all the time. Why this song comes after that one? Why you open with this particular song? And so on." He's right. Always ask yourself:

- Why are you singing those particular songs in that particular order?
- Why are you telling those anecdotes?
- Why is the band playing an instrumental in one song and not another?
- Why did you get the audience to clap along when you did?

You should know the answers to all of these questions. Singing your favourite songs just because you like them isn't enough. Each one needs to move the show along in some way and contribute to the big picture. As Barry Robinson told me, "A well crafted show has balance, pace, variety and strong links. Just throwing a list of songs together linked with banal patter is a big 'no, no'".

When you're moving from one song or section to another there needs to be a reason - a natural flow. Each part of the show should be connected to the next in some way. Don't just jump from A to D, take us through B and C first.

Everything should be done with thought and careful consideration. Everything. The way you dress, your gestures, what you say, how you move on stage, what the lights are doing and so on. Everything that happens on that stage, down to the tiniest detail, should be there for a reason. If you see a show and think it all just happens by accident, the performer has got it right. It's their job to create and recreate magic moments on stage that every audience feels are there just for them and no one else.

Be consistent but make it look spontaneous.

Director, Mark Norris, thinks it a good idea to find an artiste you admire and watch their live show a few times. "Try to find the parts that are exactly the same each time," he says, "and the parts that are left more free."

Creating magic moments

I remember seeing Lorna Luft's one woman show, 'Songs My Mother Taught Me' and being genuinely moved when she shed a tear as she told us about her childhood. I loved it so much I went back the next day. There she was hitting exactly the same spots in each song, looking surprised and humbled by the audience reaction and yes, shedding the same phoney tears. That is what theatre and crafting magic moments in a show is all about.

Of course, Luft learned from one of the greats, her mother, Judy Garland. At the end of her famous one woman show, after all the encores, the main curtains would close and as the crowd shouted for more, she would appear through the curtains wearing a white robe as though she had already changed. The audience, thinking she had been so moved by their reaction that she'd left her dressing room to come back and sing one more song, went crazy and loved her for it. Of course, it was all planned and carefully choreographed. You'll find the interview I did with Lorna Luft on the Cabaret Secrets podcast.

Barbra Streisand did a similar bit of 'business' on one of her concert tours. Pretending her new shoes were hurting her feet, she would feign embarrassment and take them off on stage. The audience loved her for being so natural and sincere. They were touched to see a huge star feel so comfortable that she would do something so familiar, like any of us would amongst good friends. Had they seen her do exactly the same bit of rehearsed shtick every other night of the tour, their hearts might not have melted quite so quickly. The same thing applies if we go back to Barbara Brussell's house party. If you'd just met your host and she was kicking her shoes off after five minutes you might think her a little presumptuous, but at the end of an evening over coffee it would be a sign that friends had been made.

Consider hiring a director

A director is someone who develops the concept for a show, briefs the technical staff, decides how the performers move and which parts of the material to emphasise. Mark Norris puts it like this, "As a director, I act as the audience. It's my job to help the performer understand how their choices affect the show. It's a collaboration."

It's like seeking help from a therapist. Sure you could just ask your friends for advice, but sometimes you need a professional opinion - someone not too close, who can give you a new perspective.

When Lennie Watts directs, he says it's his job to keep the performer, "honest, understood, and in the moment." He told me:

> It's hard to know, as a performer, how things are perceived by the audience. You know how you feel, but not necessarily how you are making us feel. Having a good director's eye can keep you on the right track. It's hard to remain objective when it's so personal. A director is that objective eye.

Jeff Harnar would agree with that. He says finding a brilliant director was the best thing he ever did:

> A director's eyes and ears can be helpful in holding up a mirror to how my onstage persona is reading out front. Adding a director was key in helping me grow from showcase rooms to major rooms and professional opportunities beyond.

When Kim Gavin's directing, he too sees the show through the eyes of the audience. Here he is on working with Donny Osmond:

> Donny is a great entertainer. Very experienced. It was really my job to be his ears in the audience. Rather than watching the show as a professional, I'd listened as a fan. I didn't need to teach him how to tell a story, he was brilliant at that, but I would help him choose the right material. I said to him, "Why don't we just look at the news every morning?" So we'd pick out stories we

liked and see how we could slot them into the show.

As far as music's concerned, it's about making a vibe happen, creating a groove and some excitement. This is something that I think has been lost for a long time. Check out the video to 'Locked Out In Heaven' by Bruno Mars. You wouldn't say they were doing choreography, but you can see he's worked with the band and they're all together creating this vibe that jumps off the stage.

With Donny, we'd find a particular song and I'd say, "This track is a groove now and you can get the whole band moving rather than just playing the song." It's not about getting them dancing - it could be something as simple as having him walk around the guitarist, step forward and have a bit of fun. Just simple interaction so they don't end up like some bands who are too scared to let go on stage.

Choose your director carefully though. Directing a cabaret artiste is quite different to working with the cast of a play or musical theatre production. If the director doesn't understand you as a performer and the essence of cabaret, they could destroy whatever magic you came with.

It's like the naturally gifted singer who takes lessons. The teacher drills them with so many scales and breathing exercises that the singer loses their unique sound. The very thing that made them special in the first place has gone. Professional advice is only any good if you choose the right professional.

If you're starting from scratch, you could collaborate with a director from day one, deciding on the show's theme, content, script and so on.

I love working with the Guildford School of Acting's musical theatre students. They are keen to learn and open to ideas. It's wonderful seeing their shows come to life after only a few weeks. So, when you find the right director, trust them and see where they take you.

If you're already performing your show, it can still be useful to work with a director to find areas of improvement. Start by explaining exactly what the show is about and the emotions you are trying to present. Talk them through each section, explaining why they're there and what you're trying to achieve. Let them watch a few performances. Be open minded and ready to try new things. Sometimes even the smallest piece of advice is enough to change your whole perspective.

Summary

Italian economist and sociologist Vilfredo Pareto found that 20% of the people owned 80% of the wealth. What became known as Pareto's principle is now widely used elsewhere. Businesses, for example, often find that 80% of sales come from 20% of clients, or 20% of product defects cause 80% of the problems. In your case, 20% of your time will go into developing 80% of your show, and 80% of the your time will go into refining it. It's those refinements that will make the difference between good and great.

- Think about every aspect of your show and always ask "Why?"
- Don't be afraid to try new things.
- If you have the budget, get professional help. It might seem expensive but consider it a long-term investment. In just a few hours a director could give you career changing advice.
- Find the Cabaret Secrets podcasts (also on YouTube) I recorded with directors like Hugh Wooldridge. They share loads of helpful advice, for free.

Secret 12: Find Your Audience

Most of this book has been about creating and perfecting your own show, but if you're working on land you'll also need to find an audience who'll pay to appreciate your hard work. Developing a fan base takes time and effort. In fact, one of the big attractions of working on a cruise ship is that your audience is already there.

A small audience means an empty room and empty pockets. If you've taken the risk and hired the venue, the musicians, the sound technician, and the publicist out of your own pocket, you could lose a lot of money. If you're lucky enough to have found someone to do that for you, they could be the one making a loss. Either way, it's a disaster that neither party will want to repeat. Save yourself the disappointment by building a fan base and press interest as soon as you can.

"Sitting Bull live by three rules: Keep bow tight, Keep arrow sharp and no put money into show business." Chief Sitting Bull, Annie Get Your Gun

Ben Walters, Cabaret Editor for Time Out London, says: "First, get good. There's no point succeeding in getting audiences and press if the work isn't what it should be. Once you're there, you should be able to articulate clearly what it is you do - the kind of material you perform, the kind of atmosphere you create, the kind of emotions you provoke - and why that combination is unique. If it isn't, you're in the wrong line."

Once you're clear about what it is you're selling, you'll need to decide whether or not to hire a publicist. Performer and cabaret champion, Hector Coris, offers some sound advice:

> Personally, I've never hired a publicist to promote my work, but I have worked alongside them in the professional theatre and cabaret community. It's expensive and – in my opinion – nebulous. If you have the hundreds, sometimes thousands, of dollars to gamble with, then have at it.
>
> I worked with a very good publicist while in the marketing department of a major off-Broadway non-profit theatre company. He had all the proper connections and channels to get the message to the right people, but ultimately, even that didn't guarantee results.
>
> You cannot blame your publicist for a small audience. Cabaret is not a Field of Dreams proposition where if you "build it, they will come." A publicist cannot (or should not) promise you an article in the New York Times, a guest spot on the local TV morning show, get your show listed in the papers or that a gaggle of reviewers will take an interest in your work. Those are certainly opportunities a press agent might be able to arrange for you, but in the end they are at the mercy of editors and producers. That's why I consider hiring a publicist a gamble.
>
> On the positive side, a good publicity agent will help you decide which avenues would be best to pursue and will often accompany you to interviews. If you do hire a publicist, my advice is two-fold:
>
> **Set a budget.** If you have the extra funds, ask the publicist what that amount can buy and explore the

options. Any good publicist will work with you and within your budgetary limitations.

Set your expectations. Having a publicist will not guarantee an audience, nor will it guarantee you'll be a media sensation. A publicist is not running around town telling people to come see your show. They are not telling people you're the greatest performer in the world and you should not be missed. I believe at the very least, a publicist will have a good mailing list to send your show information. And that could be worth spending a little money on.

I sound like I'm coming down hard on publicists, but this is only in relation to the world of cabaret. Unless you're a Broadway star making a cabaret debut or a movie actor with an intimate show, you are not news (sorry to break it to you, but someone had to say it). Cabaret gets little coverage in media (to my knowledge, there's only one print publication in the world dedicated to cabaret, Cabaret Scenes, and they only have a certain number of pages per issue) so paying a full-time publicist is one of the last places I'd recommend spending limited funds.

Cabaret is a self-propelled industry. You are your best publicist. You will work harder than any publicist you can hire to promote yourself. Do it smartly, economically and ethically.

So instead of taking a gamble with a publicist, Hector recommends a 'do it yourself' approach. He told me there's a lot you can do on your own to put yourself and your name in front of the right people, at little or no expense, to spread the word, and ultimately land you some paid work:

Network. Get involved in your local performance/cabaret community. Most large cities have their own cabaret organisations that work hard to build a community of singers, musicians, directors, etc. If not, join a cabaret group on Facebook.

It doesn't matter if you're starting out or have a somewhat established presence. If you're a newcomer it's an opportunity to meet a terrific bunch of peers and if you have a little more experience you can show you care about others.

Keep your ego in check. Don't fall into the trap of "I-saw-your-show-so-you-should-come-see-mine." Being gracious, not expecting anything in return and being an active member of the community will play out in your favour in the end.

Open Mics. Attend open mic nights. Most cities have them, but again be there as part of the community of performers and not as someone who just wants to show off. Graciousness and patience will go a long way. If you're an unfamiliar face, you may have to wait an hour or two to get up on stage. Be patient. Don't pester the host with, "When am I going on?" They may even run out of time for you. It's no secret that some open mics don't honour the sign-up order. If Liza Minnelli stops by, you can be sure that she's going on before you.

Be prepared. Most importantly, no matter what the medium of your message is (open mic, radio interview, TV appearance, etc.) you should always be prepared. Have clean music charts for the musicians (in the right key), know your lyrics. Look your best. It doesn't matter if you're doing 2-3 minutes. Those 2-3 minutes should be treated like a real, full-on performance.

You're telling people "this is just a taste of the full-hour you'll get at my complete show."

Postcards and flyers. In the cabaret world, your show postcard or flyer is your best business card. When a potential audience member stares at a huge rack of postcards and flyers or flicks through the ads in a magazine, you want yours to stand out. Your message should be strong and eye catching so people stop and read it. You want them to know what they'll get if they choose to invest an hour of their time with you.

When I design publicity material for a cabaret artiste, I start by asking them what the show is about. I want to understand the overall feeling of the show. Is it goofy, classy, moody, jazzy, more Broadway, less Broadway, etc? If you don't know what your style is, you have other things to consider than what font your name should be in. The design should look professional and well composed. The photographs or artwork should be indicative of your brand and an extension of your show.

Be smart about how you present yourself and your show to the world. If all I know about a particular performer is a really well-composed postcard, I can see they're smart enough to take the time to create a fully-realised world around their show. They just didn't slap their years-old photo on a flimsy postcard with some dates and expect people to go see it.

Get a mailing list. When I was doing musical revues, I spent many hours on the Internet scrolling through local newspaper, magazine and cabaret websites collecting the email addresses of editors, writers, reviewers and anyone else I think would be interested in what I was doing. I also hit theatre-related websites (like Playbill.com, BroadwayWorld.com etc.) who cover some cabaret. With enough digging, I had a marketing email list of over 300 emails and 5-8% of those yielded a measurable result. It was easy to do – and free!

Once you've developed a good electronic mailing list for your press releases, make sure they are well composed, error free and succinct. Professionalism is most appreciated here. Read other press releases online to help you draft your own. They can be as simple as name/date/location/short description of the show, the bios of those involved and a good photo. Be short and sweet and at the very least, you may get a mention in the event listings.

Set up a Google Alert (or similar catch system) for your name so you don't have to scour all these publications online to see if your show is mentioned. Let Google find it for you. You'll be surprised where your show info will pop up.

Print Media

When it comes to exploiting print media, Time Out's Ben Walters says:

> To get press coverage, send information about your show well in advance and check the outlet's website or listings information so you can give them what they need in the first place rather than making them chase you for missing information. And get pictures. Good pictures. At an early career stage, a so-so act with great pictures will find it easier to get coverage than a great act with so-so pictures.

As Hector Coris pointed out, there is only one magazine in the world dedicated to cabaret and according to Mark Shenton, "In London, the only print media to regularly review the field is The Times, The Stage and Time Out." Consequently, he offers some great advice: "Concentrate on getting audiences, not reviews."

People like Mark and Ben are deluged with requests for artistes vying for attention. I asked Ben to explain how he chooses which acts he'll give valuable column inches to:

> Originality, excellence or audience expectation. If an act is unfamiliar to me but intriguing in their press material (or perhaps glimpses of their work I've seen in other people's shows or online), and I don't think I've seen anything quite like it, I'll be motivated to check it out. If I know a performer has done work to a very high standard in the past, I'll be curious about what they're doing next. And if I think readers will already be curious about a show, I'll want to provide them with an account of it, even if I don't expect it to be especially original or excellent.

To build audiences, Ben suggests, "spend time collecting emails, Facebook friends and Twitter followers."

Founder of Musical Theatre Review, Lisa Martland is a well-known critic. I asked her how people like us can impress people like her:

> There needs to be a reason why a reviews commissioner is going to choose you, rather than the oodles of others who are sending their information.
>
> It sounds boring, but performers need to know in advance how much notice newspapers, magazines, radio and TV stations need to put the show in their

listings pages and what information they require in order to consider reviewing the show. The more information and notice you give, the more likely it is that someone will be sent along. The venue cannot be relied on for this.

If there is anything particularly topical about the show, or the artiste in question has just appeared in a West End production, or has something else on their CV that might make them a more attractive prospect, then all that should be used for promotion.

If there's a good quote from a previous review that can be used, that can help too. Find out the name of the person you need to communicate with, it will get to him or her quicker and the person in question will see you have taken the trouble to find out. And, of course, don't send the information to loads of publications that would never review cabaret in the first place. Research is important in this respect as well.

Social Media

The sooner an artiste is ready to build an online following, the sooner they can start filling cabaret rooms. Mark Shenton says:

> More than anything nowadays, social media is a cheap and highly effective tool for self-marketing. I once went to see Lee Lessack at the Pizza on the Park - a good American singer with zero celebrity profile - but the place was packed. At one point, he said, 'You all look much bigger than your Facebook pictures!' That's how he got his audience. Of course, you can't just create a Facebook profile and Twitter account and feel your job is done. It needs serious work to build friends and followers.

Lisa Martland agrees:

> Self-promotion online has become vital nowadays via Twitter, Facebook, LinkedIn (don't forget this one, it can be really useful on a professional basis), as well as the artiste having their own website.

I asked Phil Barley, co-founder of online marketing consultancy DigitalSurgeon.co.uk, the best way to build a following on Facebook:

> Be yourself and be consistent. Being yourself is very important because Facebook users are real people and so are you. If you have an opinion on something, especially if it is your area of expertise, you should share it and encourage debate. If you don't have a stand-point, your followers won't know much about you and will soon lose interest.
>
> The recommended minimum amount of Facebook updates to grow a following is around one each day. They don't have to be ground-breaking but it does help if they are remarkable, and by that I mean, worth remarking on.
>
> Sharing great content, especially video and pictures, is a good way to gain more Likes, so it's worth subscribing to online blogs and magazines that write about your subject, and then share their news.
>
> Be a curator of interesting information that will benefit your followers. A good tip is to use Google Alerts to set up a constant search for any mention about the things you like to share. For example, I founded TheatreDigsBooker.com, an online accommodation

resource for film and theatre professionals, so we use alerts like "theatre tour UK".

I asked Phil, which is better, Twitter or Facebook:

> They work well together but if you were to choose only one, I'd say Twitter elicits more engagement than Facebook. Twitter is open to anyone whereas only your followers can view your feed on Facebook.
>
> With Twitter, the best advice is to treat it like a cocktail party: If you were out to mingle and meet new people and someone walked straight up to you and told you all about their business and what they have for sale you would probably excuse yourself as quickly as possible. It's polite to ask questions and take an interest in other people and when the conversation naturally leads there, one can introduce the business element (it helps to match benefits to needs if you already know their needs). Treat Twitter the same way: follow people (to join in the conversation) and offer help and advice if you have it, otherwise stay quiet.
>
> Learn to understand the language of Twitter and follow the 'give much more that you take' idea. In other words, join in with conversations, answer questions, offer solutions, retweet other people's tweets and help promote other people before you ask them for anything in return - you're much more likely to get a positive response when you ask, "Could you retweet this for me?"

Most of us are pretty busy as it is. The thought of spending even more time at a computer, especially when I'm on the road, is not one I relish. I asked Phil how much time anyone should expect to spend building and maintaining a profile:

> With free tools like Later and Hootsuite, you can schedule your posts to go out at whatever time you like (or at automatically optimised times). This means you can spend one afternoon a week scheduling updates for the whole week. Then, throughout the week, you can concentrate on listening and answering questions rather than trying to find something new to say every day.
>
> Unless you can make something that instantly goes viral, you should expect to take 6-12 months to build a useful following.

Interacting with friends and fans online can be fun, but I've often wondered how many of my followers actually buy my music or come to a show. I asked Phil if there's any point in having thousands of followers who might never spend any money. He told me:

> Kevin Kelly writes about "One thousand true fans" in his famous blog post. He suggests that if you have one thousand people who share what you produce, buy your concert tickets and every record you make then you will never need to worry about money again. What he means is, if the people who follow you find what you do or say interesting enough, they will share it, and consequently, become your sales force.
>
> You can buy 10,000 followers for £5 on some websites but that will do you absolutely no good whatsoever. You're much better off having 250 true fans as followers who engage, discuss, share and comment than you are ten thousand people who only

click Like or Follow and never come back.

Musician, Harry the Piano, thinks that if you work hard to build up your profile it will generate income, but he told me:

> You do need a hell of a lot of friends/fans/followers to impact sales. It is a great marketing option but I wouldn't recommend spending hours and hours on it unless it's your primary promotion tool. A good, self-updatable website with an interactive mailing list is of just as much value. If you're a performer you should be constantly replying to people who like your stuff or who express an interest. Ask for their email address and send just four or five missives a year. Keep them light and short (no deluge of details), and try to hone them to only the really good stuff you're doing.

Harry knows what he's talking about. His YouTube videos have attracted well over 3 million views. I wanted to know how he did it, was it talent or did he just get lucky?

> I was urged onto YouTube by the worry that 95% of my audience was approaching... well...95, and had the intention of generating more youthful interest. I tried to do something that no one else really does: playing in different styles spontaneously requested. I thought it might do moderately well but was dumbstruck by how it turned out.
>
> The initial spike came from a feature on some US cable show then it just took off. It was featured on Reddit, which generated 70,000 views in one day. Hits just generate more and more hits. If you have a talent to display you are 10% there. In my opinion the other 90%

is thinking long and hard about how to present that in an entertaining, amusing and above all unusual way. Po-faced playing/singing/juggling just won't hack it, even if you are the next Elvis!

It's massively worth the effort. A smartphone, a friend and a YouTube account equals zero overheads. I've had job offers worldwide from that one clip alone. Respond to all messages, reply to enquiries and befriend those that want to join in. This isn't Facebook, so there are no real consequences. That's what I did and I now have over 9,000 subscribers.

As for building a following on Twitter, Harry says:

Start by following a couple of hundred big names: actors, comics, politicians etc., anyone who even vaguely appeals. That instantly puts you in the heart of the Twitter-sphere. Then tweet as often and as amusingly/interestingly as possible. They say an average of three tweets a day is the optimum. Oh, and if you're replying to something personal or mundane, don't tweet, 'Yeah, ok see you at 7,' Direct Message it!

Your website

Take a quick glance over any performer's website and you'll find that they are the "most exciting", "most talented" and generally "the most remarkable" talent that ever walked the earth. Every click of the mouse reveals yet more testimonials bursting with superlatives. Having complete editorial control over your own website is like being the dictator of a small country. At the push of a button you can silence dissenting voices and keep everything just the way you like it. Goebbels would be proud.

Curb your hyperbole

My advice is to stick to plain language and useful information. Bookers are looking for the meat. They don't have time to wade through flowery language to find out what you've done and what you can do for them. They know the more decent credits you have, the less you need to pad your bio with hyperbole.

Agent friendly

Include high-resolution photos that can be easily downloaded for bookers and clients to use in publicity. Avoid too much animation on the site. Make sure all the main text can be easily copied and pasted by anyone who wants it. Give your showreel pride of place - it's the main selling tool. Agent, Jo Martin says:

> It's important for an act to have an 'agent friendly' website. This means it shouldn't show the act's contact details, only the agent. Why would an agent send a potential booker to the website only for him to go ahead and contact the act direct?
>
> An artiste expects loyalty from his agent and agents expect it from their acts. It works both ways. Occasionally an artiste thinks they can save themselves some commission, but ultimately the agent will find out and it can cost the artiste much more in the long run.

Web designer, Carlos Castillo, offers some useful advice for anyone about to create their own website:

> Think about your website (and social network sites) from the point of view of your audience. Ask yourself what sort of site would they like to see and build the structure and your narrative around that.

Look around for inspiration. Spend a few hours browsing websites and social media profiles and make notes of anything you find inspiring. It's not about copying other people, but bringing ideas from different places to develop your own style. Don't limit yourself to checking similar artists. The best inspiration often comes from people, companies and products from many different areas.

When you've found a web designer you want to work with, the first step is to compile all your content (copy and images). Having everything prepared beforehand will help you decide the best way to structure and present your new site.

I normally ask my clients for a Word document with the site structure (a list of sections, subsections, etc.) and different documents for each section's copy. Then a folder with all the images and media (sound and video) to be included. Ideally, the files should be clearly labelled or separated into sub-folders. Images, audio files and videos should not be too small/compressed. If necessary I can easily reduce the file sizes but it's impossible to increase.

If you want to use video on your site, I normally recommend you upload your files to your Vimeo or YouTube account. Once you give me the links, I can load the files to your website directly from there.

Decide how often you expect to update the content on your website. This will help your designer to decide whether it's worth setting up a Content Management System (like Wordpress, which will allow you to update content by yourself), or if you're better off with a 'static' site which is cheaper to set up but more difficult for you to edit later.

A popular alternative for anyone unwilling to invest in a CMS straightaway, is to setup a static site that display feeds from social media sites like Facebook and Twitter. This helps to keep the site fresh and relevant and though not ideal, it could be a good starting point if your budget is limited.

As Carlos says, to keep people interested it's important update the site regularly. These days there are some amazing and low cost options for creating your own site, like SquareSpace, Google Sites and Wix. It's fast and easy.

Summary

Every artiste needs an audience. You are your best publicist so unless you've got deep pockets to hire help, start building your fan base now.

- First, perfect your act and know what you are trying to say.
- Work with a good graphic designer to develop branding and powerful, attention-grabbing publicity material.
- Network. Get out as much as possible. Go to cabaret events, clubs, open mics and join your local cabaret organisations. Meet people, make friends and get known.
- Build a mailing list of fans and media contacts. Keep your emails occasional, short and sweet.
- Be realistic about print media.
- Exploit social media for all it's worth.

Secret 13: Rock Stars Live Like Nuns

Your voice is your livelihood, your artistic outlet and your pay check. I never used to give mine a second thought but like anything else you take for granted, you only miss it when it's gone.

I never really had any problems until a few years ago. I began to notice my throat feeling sore and fatigued after only one or two shows. Concerned, I saw a specialist who put a camera down my throat to see what was going on. I'd been shown models of the throat before, but seeing my own vocal folds, uvula and tonsils in action was far more impactful than a piece of moulded plastic. It was good news. There was no damage to my throat and I didn't have nodes. He sent me to a speech therapist whose advice was simple, but profound. "You are not," she said, with all the tact of a sledgehammer, "twenty anymore. You cannot abuse your voice as you used to and expect to get away with it."

Beyond the obvious importance of avoiding smoky places and warming up before singing, she gave me some very useful advice. Sometimes it's good to be reminded of the simple things.

Avoid noisy environments

The noisier the place, the louder we speak. This can strain our voices leaving us tired and hoarse. Even talking loudly on a mobile phone where there's background noise can be tiring. I always avoid noisy bars and clubs the night before I have a show. To be honest, I rarely socialise at all the night before I work. It's boring, I know, but the strain on my voice isn't worth it.

Speak softly and stand straight
I have learned to speak more quietly in day-to-day conversation. To save unnecessary wear on my vocal chords I try to talk less (a challenge for someone like me), face the person I'm addressing and think twice before shouting across a room. The Alexander Technique's been helpful too in finding an upright, neutral posture.

Keep hydrated
The vocal folds need to be well lubricated to vibrate efficiently, so drink lots of water. Caffeine and alcohol pull water out of our bodies so should be drunk in moderation. I avoid alcohol completely the night before I perform. Air conditioning, especially on airplanes, can also leave the throat feeling dry so make-up for it by drinking extra water.

Avoid throat clearing and coughing
Coughing to clear mucus from the throat can be damaging to the vocal chords and should be avoided. Instead, try clearing the throat with a long, sharp breath as if you're sounding an "H" while you exhale.

Maintain good general health
I usually make time for some kind of daily exercise. If I get to the gym, I try not to sweat too much and only lift weights if they're small and pastel coloured. If I'm honest, I go for two reasons: cake and vanity. The more weight I lose in the gym the more cake I can eat. As it happens though, there are other benefits to

taking care of yourself.

Regular exercise and a healthy diet help us feel better for longer. This is more than just vanity. We're less likely to suffer a blocked nose or sore throat and we'll recover quicker after illness. We also need to be in good physical shape to maintain sufficient stamina for our shows and all the travelling we have to do. Jet-lag and switching time zones can be gruelling. If you don't fancy the gym, stretching at home or a good walk will do the job.

Don't take your health for granted. Get all the sleep you need and try to get plenty of exercise. You'll look healthier, sound better and feel more energised. Cake is optional.

Warming Up and Cooling Down

Sam West is one of London's most respected vocal experts. I've been using his warm-up CD for about seven years, usually for twenty minutes the day before my show and again on the day itself. I asked him if he thought that was enough:

> Every singer and every job has different requirements for warm ups. Some gigs may need a lot of singing in wide areas of the range, and others may be more straightforward. About 30 mins of warming up should be sufficient in most cases. Actually, I know some singers who don't even warm up at all, but they know their voices very well and exactly what they can or can't get away with!

Singer and vocal coach, Michael Dore, says it's really important to warm the voice up in stages:

> It wakes up the vocal muscles, prepares them for what's ahead and builds the stamina. Singers are like

athletes. A runner would never race without preparing and warming up the muscles. We're vocalising gymnasts!

Don't sleep heavily before your show. The voice tends to go to sleep again, so rest, but not too heavily just before a performance.

The late Jeannie Deva was an international voice and performance coach with a career that spanned nearly five decades. I once asked her for some advice on how to keep our voices sounding better for longer and she generously let me share these tips and exercises from her book 'The Contemporary Vocalist':

The production of your voice is dependent not only on breath, but on the coordinated and small movements of many muscles. External muscles of your rib cage and throat, as well as internal muscles of your larynx, tongue, inner throat, and soft palate, to name but a few, must not only be in good tone, but must be prepared each time, prior to demanding use.

Everyone is different. Your warm-up routines may need to vary on a day to day basis, according to the nature of the performance or rehearsal. The time of day, condition of your body, and the condition of your voice also influence your warm-up. Some singers develop an exact, never varying routine that fits their needs no matter what. However, the more tools you have, the better you will be able to create the right warm-up routine each time.

With a proper vocal warm-up done, you will be able to start your rehearsals or performances in your best shape, rather than risk a blown out voice. The idea is to stretch, tone, and limber your vocal muscles so that they are ready to respond to your needs. This is true whether you are a singer or actor. Treat your voice with respect.

Warm-ups help you save, not wreck your voice, assisting performance excellence and career longevity.

Your Breathing

Your body's breathing mechanism plays a major role in singing. The following exercise is the first in a series designed to stretch and tone muscles that are vital to this important function. Throughout this exercise keep your mouth open and throat relaxed so that your breathing is unrestricted and occurs naturally in response to the stretch and release of your ribs.

- Stand relaxed but erect, with your arms hanging by either side.
- Turn your palms forward, facing the wall directly in front of your body.
- Open your mouth slightly and keep it open and relaxed throughout the entire exercise.
- Stretch your arms up and out to the sides of your body as you slowly raise them. It will be as though you are drawing a large arc with your fingertips around the sides of your body. (As you stretch your arms out and up, air will naturally inhale through your open mouth).
- As you continue stretching and raising, your arms will stretch up from your shoulders. Let them angle slightly forward along the sides of your face and bring your palms together as though you were going to dive into a pool. Your out-stretched arms will lift your shoulders and elongate your back

muscles. Your face should be forward not raised. If your stomach is tense, let it relax. Keep your mouth open and relaxed.
- Silently count to six while continuing to stretch up.
- Keep your mouth open and throat relaxed. Do not breathe in or out.
- Now let your arms down faster than you raised them. Bring them down the same way you brought them up. Your breath should naturally exhale through your open mouth as you lower your arms.
- Repeat steps one through seven for a total of twenty repetitions. After doing each ten repetitions take a few minutes rest. Done daily, this will take about fifteen to twenty minutes.

Face and Neck Massage
Your sound is made inside your throat by the varied vibration of your vocal folds. Relaxed muscles of the neck permit the inner vocal muscles to move with greater ease.

Reflect on some pleasant thought or memory, or just take on a peaceful state of mind. As you do each step, breathe slowly and deeply.

Begin by massaging the muscles of your face. With the fingers of both hands, start at the top centre of your forehead. Using a circular motion, massage down both sides of your forehead to your ears. Massage your jaw in front of your ears, and then your cheeks, under your eyes and chin. Concentrate your massage on these areas until you can feel the muscles soften and relax.

Next massage the muscles of your neck. Use the fingers of both hands. Start just under the back of your head. On either side of your spine, stroke down to your shoulders in one smooth or several short motions. Continue until relaxed.

From the back of your neck, use a few fingers of each hand and begin stroking forward to the sides of your neck. Repeat this motion as many times as necessary, until you feel the muscles relax.

Beginning just behind your jaw on both sides of your neck, stroke downwards to your shoulders. Repeat as many times as you wish. Work slowly and carefully. Continue until any soreness is gone.

With the fingers of both hands, use a short forward stroke on the muscles directly below and under the corners of your jaw. As you feel them relax, work forward to under your chin. Repeat this from the corners of your jaw. Do not push or poke. Maintain a slow, gentle touch and don't forget to breath.

Tongue Relaxer

Singing and speaking with relaxed muscles at the back of the tongue plays an important part in your voice sounding resonant and free. These next exercises will help to improve the tone and projection of your voice. Open your mouth slightly. Slowly stretch your tongue out and down while letting it remain relaxed. When extended as far forward as possible, slowly stretch it over to one side.

Return it to its stretched and forward position. Slowly stretch it to the other side. Return it to the centre stretch. Now slowly retract it into your mouth.

Swallow. Do this sequence only once or twice. It can be repeated later in the day, but don't overdo it. The tongue is a muscle and can be strained.

Lip Trills

Although this may at first feel silly to do, this exercise provides a wonderful massage for your entire vocal tract (specifically lips, cheeks, tongue, soft palate, the back wall of your throat, and larynx). We will be using vibration to massage your inner instrument. If you have a tendency to tense your throat muscles when singing or speaking, this can help.

- Take a breath.
- With your lips lightly together, slowly and gently exhale just enough so your lips begin flapping like a motor boat's engine.
- Do this for as long as you can.
- Take a breath and repeat. Work on lengthening the amount of time you can do this on one breath. When you have repeated this several times successfully, your lip and cheek muscles should feel energised and relaxed.

Sustained Hums

Take a deep breath, expanding your back open side to side. Maintain that rib elevation with the muscles of the back of your sides while you gently hum a pitch in your mid range. Do this for as long as you can.

Time yourself with the second hand of a clock. See how many seconds you can sustain the hum. Repeat several times.

Resonance Wake-Up

This warm up does as its name suggests - it wakes up the resonance of your voice. It's also excellent for examining and developing the basic vowel sounds used in singing.

This exercise uses a series of different vowel to consonant combinations. As you do this, use a basic speaking volume only, on a comfortable midrange pitch.

The consonant will be an "NG". You shape this consonant with the back of your tongue and soft palate. The back of your tongue raises and lightly meets your soft palate. To find this, say the word "sing" and sustain the "NG" position at the end of the word.

- Take a breath. With your mouth kept slightly open and unmoving, rest the tip of your tongue against the back of your bottom teeth.
- Put the back of your tongue in the "NG" position and begin sustaining a comfortable midrange pitch.
- Feel the vibration shimmer along the roof of your mouth.
- Sustaining the same pitch, change to an "AH" vowel (pronounced as in "wand"). The back of your tongue will naturally lower and relax as you sustain the "AH" vowel.
- On the same breath, alternate from the "NG" consonant with the vowel as many times as you can, NG-AH, NG-AH, NG-AH, etc.
- Repeat using the same vowel until you experience muscle relaxation in the back of your mouth and throat. Then go to the next NG-vowel combination.

The sequence goes as follows:

- NG-AH (Wand)

- NG-EE (Seem)
- NG-A (Same)
- NG-AA (Apple)
- NG-Eh (When)
- NG-Uh (Some)
- NG-I (Him)

During the next two, be sure you do not shape your lips for the sound. This can be achieved by thinking the vowel sound and letting it naturally resonate against the back wall of your mouth/throat.

- NG-Oh (Home)
- NG-Ooo (Soon)

Vocal Cool-Downs
I have heard many singers complain of vocal fatigue and huskiness after a gig. They were confused as to what they were doing wrong. They were warming up beforehand and working correctly with their voice while singing. They could hear themselves in the monitors and weren't straining, so why did they have vocal fatigue or a husky voice? This situation was corrected by five to ten minutes of cool-down exercises immediately after their performance.

To return to the athlete analogy again, a runner wouldn't just stop and sit down after completing a marathon or short sprint. They walk and gently stretch until their muscles have returned to normal. Your vocal muscles are small and subtle compared to the ones in a runner's legs, but they undergo a similar workout when you sing or do a lot of vocal exercises. You can reduce the chance of vocal fatigue and huskiness by using a cool-down to return your vocal folds to their everyday speaking condition.

The Lip Trills, mentioned above, also work well as a cool-down. In fact, any basic vocal exercises that can be used for vocal warm-up can serve for cool-down.

Another simple cool-down exercise is to slide your voice through a series of five notes, using an "Ah" or an "Ee" vowel sound. Gently slide from the root (tonic) of a scale up to the fifth (e.g. C up to G) and back back down to the root imitating the sound of a siren. Continue this small slide climbing slightly higher each time and then sliding down to slightly lower tonic. In this way you will be starting lower and ending higher, stretching the range of the siren.

Do not be concerned with range though and use a very easy relaxed speaking volume. If you find it difficult to do lip trills or other vocal exercises immediately after your rehearsal or gig, sing an easy song at a low (but not whispered) volume.

As for how long we should spend warming up and cooling down, Jeannie further recommends:

> A warm-up routine can last anywhere from ten to thirty minutes. Cool-down is usually five to ten minutes, but should be continued until you notice a difference. Your speaking voice should sound normal again and feel comfortable.
>
> If you are a bit self-conscious about doing these cool-downs in front of others, just remember that professionals do what it takes to sound great and prolong their careers. You will just have to overcome any embarrassment and do the cool-downs to satisfy

the needs of your vocal muscles to maintain vocal health and longevity.

There are differences of opinion. Sam West doesn't believe a vocal cool down is necessary. He says:

> After using the voice a lot for a performance regular talking is enough to get back to normal. Sometimes, if the work is intense, it would actually be better to rest and avoid using the voice at all. This is especially true if the voice is going to be used a lot again in the near future.

Personally, I do both. I'll hum gently for a few minutes after coming off stage and then try to avoid talking too much for the rest of the night, especially if I have to sing again the next day.

Everyone's different. Depending on physicality, workload, time and practicality, I think it's for each of us to find our own routine of effective vocal care. Just don't take it for granted. As Jeannie says, "Treat your voice with respect." Do that, and you'll sing better for longer.

Jazz singer and voice coach at the London College of Music, Iain Mackenzie, thinks that good vocal care is all about the simple things:

> The most important thing for me when I'm busy is a very slow, consistent warm-up and gentle cool-down. Drink loads of water and very little alcohol. Stick to a regular eating routine and get plenty of sleep. Most of all don't get stressed about loosing your voice as it's guaranteed that if you do, you will!

What if you have a sore throat?

A sore throat can be the first sign of a common cold, flu, laryngitis and worse. Bacteria or viruses can infect the throat and tonsils, causing unpleasant inflammation and making singing a struggle. For the professional singer, the feeling you get when you just know you have a sore throat coming on, is both unsettling and mildly annoying.

The most common causes of a sore throat are both infectious and non-infectious. A virus such as the common cold or a bacterial infection like strep-throat, acid reflux or GERD (Gastroesophageal reflux disease) can cause pharyngitis, a nasty inflammation at the back of your throat, whilst non- infectious cases typically come from things like air pollution, allergies or smoking. In any case, they all can drastically affect the physical make-up of the vocal folds thus manifesting in some unwanted discomfort when attempting to sing.

Richard Halton, vocal coach and co-founder of Vocal Balance, spent years singing in opera houses and in the West End. How did he cope with having to sing on a sore throat?

> In my career, I have been in many a compromising situation having to go onstage suffering from varying degrees of sore throat. Sometimes, prior to a performance I tried every known remedy to man: gargling salty water, drinking very cold liquids, downing a teaspoon of olive oil, even eating copious amounts of liquorice. The general rule is: if you catch it early enough you can avert problems down the line. Singing on a sore throat in truth can cause more problems than it solves.
>
> When it comes to singing for your supper you simply don't have time to get sick, so during 'sore throat season' I find it isn't always enough to suck on

your favourite throat lozenges or to drink flavoured teas, but to have a few more tried and tested remedies at your disposal. A few years ago when I was working in the West End, a colleague recommended a slippery Chinese syrup called 'Nin Jiom Pei Pa Koa.' Thought to have anti-inflammatory properties, this syrup has, on numerous occasions, saved my proverbial bacon, during shows. It feels like it coats the throat and provides an antidote to that horrible sensation of swallowing razor-blades.

Many pro-singers and swear by ginger in its various forms - even eating whole chunks - which can soothe and bring down swelling. Another popular incarnation includes a hot brew of honey, lemon and ginger, which is very soothing and helps calm a potentially excitable neurosis.

The truth is, there are so many different solutions to throat scratchiness or soreness ranging from Throat Coat tea, nasal to cleansing salts, Manuka honey to off-the-shelf throat lozenges. But, whenever possible, the best and most proven remedy for a sore-throat is quite simply a vow of silence.

Michael Dore agrees that prevention is always better than cure. As he told me:

> I do my best to avoid a sore throat happening in the first place. I try to live healthily. I watch my diet, exercise, get plenty of sleep and always wrap up well when going out in the cold. At the first sign of a sore throat I go for warm honey and lemon drinks. I've found that if I act quickly, a sore throat can be prevented.

He's right. If you listen to your body and act quickly, you might be able to nip illness in the bud. A bacterial infection like strep throat can come on suddenly with a high fever. It can be highly contagious and you should see a doctor. If it's a virus with little or no fever, there's no point in taking antibiotics. Instead, at the first sign of illness, rest, gargle homemade remedies and drink lots of water or soothing warm drinks.

Singer, Eleanor Keenan swears by fresh pineapple juice. I prefer to gargle with warm salt water and drink lots of hot water with freshly squeezed lemon, honey, ginger and a dash of Tabasco.

There are bound to be times when regardless of how rough you might be feeling, the show must go on. "If your throat's sore when you have a performance," says Michael, "you just have to do your best. A gentle warm up is still good but don't overwork the voice, you might not be able to sing some of those notes too often, so don't exhaust yourself in the warm up."

After my first week performing as Sinatra in the West End's 'Rat Pack' show, I lost my voice. I'd been rehearsing for weeks, was stressed and exhausted. After the last show of the week I went out to celebrate. My voice was already tired, but after a late, noisy, boozy night on the town, I woke on Sunday to find I had no voice at all. Nothing. It was terrifying. My manager sent me to his Harley Street doctor whose patients have included some of the biggest names in show-business including, ironically enough, Sinatra himself. He started by giving me a good dressing down for thinking I could party like that while in the middle of West End run and expect to get away with it. He advised complete vocal rest and his "three, three, three cure": gargle three times a day for three minutes with 300 mgs of soluble Disprin. After a week, I was fully recovered and back to work, but I'd learned my lesson.

I never forgot what he told me that day: "Don't be fooled by the all night party image rock stars like to promote. Whatever they say, the real stars are consummate pros," he said, "when they're working, they live like nuns."

Secret 14: How To Get An Agent

Some acts with plenty of experience represent themselves, but that's unusual; most have an agent. Good representation means you don't have to maintain relationships with lots of people - you deal with your agent and they take care of everything else. They'll entertain bookers, agree contracts and make sure you get paid. Aside from everything else, having a good agent will enhance your image and open doors.

Let's look at how to get an agent and what to expect when you find one.

Get a personal recommendation
You could browse the Internet or industry reference books like Artists & Agents, Contacts or The White Book to find bookers and agents. Without a personal recommendation, though, you might be wasting your time.

My agent receives up to 300 unsolicited emails every week from artistes hungry for work. They range from solo instrumentalists, speciality acts, duos, vocalists, groups, classical acts and production singers, all with established acts looking for new opportunities. Most of them, sadly, will have to keep on looking.

Mark Eynon, Director of the Newbury Spring Festival, is typical in his approach:

> I rarely book an artiste I've not heard live, though I do make exceptions if they come highly recommended by

a trusted colleague or reputable manager.

For cabaret especially, personality is key and you can rarely capture it in a recording unless it's a very well produced showreel. Beyond that, I'm looking for musical talent, box office appeal and reliable professional management who don't send me too much to read and don't expect an immediate answer.

It's unlikely I'll take a direct approach from an artiste seriously, unless it is supported by an endorsement from someone I respect.

Give yourself a head start. Ask around. If you know other artistes, see which agents they use. What you really need is a personal recommendation. Without that, your chances of being noticed are slim.

Getting noticed

Using an act for the first time can be risky for a booker. I wanted to find out how they decide which artistes they can trust.

Ruth Leon, former Artistic Director for the prestigious Crazy Coqs cabaret room in London's West End, told me:

> I have no amour propre when it comes to bookings. I can't know every artiste out there, so often rely on those whose taste and discrimination I trust. I get ideas from agents, listening to the radio and recommendations from colleagues and other artistes.
>
> I never book an artiste I haven't heard and usually seen. Otherwise, everybody's mother would recommend a constant stream of mediocrity.
>
> There is so much that I look for - innate talent, experience in front of an audience, taste when preparing a programme, and ease with the public.

Above all, I look at the way the artiste relates to the audience. If they can't make direct contact with everyone, making them an essential part of the show, it doesn't matter how beautiful the voice or intelligent the patter.

An artiste unknown to me, presenting themselves and asking for work, has to do a lot more than tell me how good they are. I want a bio, a photograph or two, a CD or showreel, an indication of what their show is about and how they want to present it in my venue. If an artiste doesn't know the territory, they won't get through the door.

Clive Thomas produces events for private parties and corporate clients. When we chatted, he was in Ecuador checking every detail ahead of a group he was taking out there. "I leave nothing to chance," he told me:

On some occasions I might take a recommendation from another performer whose standards are as high as mine, but that's rare. My clients have high expectations and it's my job to make sure they are met. A good showreel is the first step. If I like that I'll go see the artiste perform, or at least meet them in person.

Even if you can't see them work, meeting someone gives you a good idea of what they might be like to work with.

I remember hearing an incredible young tenor and thought he'd be perfect for one of our special musical evenings. I met him and immediately knew we just wouldn't get along. I was right. He went on to work for lots of producers, but never more than once. I've since heard this gifted but arrogant performer became a lorry driver. A terrible waste, but proof that talent isn't everything.

The Electronic Press Kit

My agent, Gary Parkes, told me, "It would have been okay spending the money on a glossy brochure ten years ago but now there's no point. If we sent them to our clients they'd just be ignored; everybody's so busy." He prefers artists to email an EPK. An Electronic Press Kit is the digital equivalent of a brochure, DVD, photos and bio.

Don't send anything blind. Call first, explaining who you are and that you want to send some publicity material. Ask for the name of the person you should send it to and their email address. If they refuse to give you a name, ask for a general email address.

Send a short email introducing yourself and explaining what you do and what you want.

- Include a YouTube link to your showreel. Don't send video files - they are too big and might not be compatible with the booker's computer. Your showreel is your single most important marketing tool.
- Attach one or two publicity photos and your set lists. Use Microsoft Word or PDFs.
- Include your biography. Unless you're using direct quotes from reviewers, avoid going overboard with superlatives like, "A stunning performer" and "Guaranteed to leave everyone awestruck with her remarkable talent". Here's a tip to make sure your bio isn't drowning in its own magnificence. Invite a few friends over, give them a copy of your bio and ask them to read it out loud to your face. If they can get through it without laughing, it's probably okay.

- Agents may check references so don't exaggerate your credits.

My agent says he does at least glance at every email he receives. If something jumps out at him he'll be straight on the phone to talk to the act and arrange a face-to-face meeting.

If you don't get an immediate response, I suggest you wait a week and follow up with a phone call or another email. Polite Persistence Pays. Even if you get a "no" now, email them again in a few months time. Things are always changing so send occasional follow-up emails and include your YouTube link again. You never know when a booker will be looking for an act just like yours.

Your email should have an attention grabbing subject line. Give the agent a reason to read your email instead of someone else's. What's in it for them? They don't care if you've recorded a nice CD or won a local talent competition. This is business. They want to earn lots of easy commission from acts so good their clients are fighting to book them. They want an easy life with artistes who don't waste their time, who get back to them quickly and who stick to their commitments.

My style might not be right for you, but here's the kind of email I would send if I was starting out:

> **Subject:** He SINGS, plays the SAX and speaks THREE LANGUAGES!
> OR
> **Subject:** Star of the West End's 'Rat Pack' is ready and willing...
> Dear [name of agent]
> I know you get bombarded with emails from acts all the time, but wait... click here and watch 30 seconds of my showreel. I promise it will be worth your while.

"Michael Bublé is not the only singer keeping the Sinatra flame alive." The Sunday Times

I have 2 x 50 minute shows designed for cabaret rooms, parties and cruise ships. I specialise in Sinatra but include something for everyone including songs in Spanish, Portuguese, German and Japanese. My bio, set lists and photos are attached.

I'm looking for exclusive representation. I have no manager to get in the way (you'll deal directly with me), have lots of availability and will gladly consider anything.

Call me on xxxx xxxxx or email me.

I look forward to hearing from you soon.

Gary Williams

www.garywilliams.co.uk

Get a great showreel

Like everyone I spoke to, Hector Coris thinks a showreel is essential. "90% of the time I'm considering seeing a performer I don't know, I'll look online for video clips. Audio clips can work too, but the visual is also part of the experience. Make sure it looks good though; I've skipped seeing some performers based on a terrible video they posted of themselves."

Manager and agent Jo Martin told me:

> A showreel is vital. Years ago potential bookers would usually go and see an act in person, but that's all changed. These days we're dealing with bookers all over the world and a showreel crosses that divide. Unless you're a well established act, it's almost impossible to get work without a good showreel. Sometimes just 5 or 10 minutes of the show is enough, but it needs to be presented professionally - it could be

the most important ten minutes of your career!

She's not alone. Every booker I spoke to says in most cases it's the showreel that get's the work. It stands to reason that it's worth spending the time and money to get it right. It should be around 5 to 10 minutes long, show a good range of songs, audience interaction and chat. You can see mine at garywilliams.co.uk

If you're working on land and you're ready to get your show filmed, you'll have little choice but to hire a venue, a band, publicise your show, get an audience along, hire a professional sound and lighting team and pay a video production company to film the whole thing and edit it. You can easily spend thousands and still end up with a weak showreel. I know, I've done it.

If you're already working on a ship, everything you need is right there under your nose. You have a ready-made audience, a great venue with state of the art lighting (usually far better than what you'll find on land), excellent musicians, and so on. Just get a friend or the onboard video production team to film it, and look after everyone who's helping you. Those of you already working on ships as production singers have a clear advantage over most people so make the most of it while you can.

Get a gimmick

Got an agent already? Think they should be getting you more work, more money and giving you more attention? Don't be too quick to fire them. They can only book what's in demand and in recent years entertainment budgets have been cut and good work is harder to find. Instead of complaining and blaming your agent, learn some new skills and give your act the edge. In a market flooded with good acts, bookers are always on the look out for something different. Marketeers call it a USP, a Unique

Sales Point. There are thousands of singers looking for work, but one who also plays saxophone or speaks fluent German will stand out from the crowd.

Find out what people want then give it to them.

Maria King is a classically trained pianist who plays Mahler with consummate ease and looks the model of sophistication in her stunning couture. The trouble is, she's not the only one. As good as she is, there are many more just like her. It's only when she surprises everyone with her self-effacing humour, rich accent, and a repertoire that includes jazz, boogie-woogie and comedy vocal pieces, that we understand why she's so successful.

Sharon López is flamenco dancer. Her husband, Máté Rácz is a violinist. They are both world-class performers, and for years, had solid careers working in shows created by other people. When they decided to team-up and create their own show, everything changed. Their act was so different to anything else out there that, in record time, they had a packed schedule, headlining all over the world.

There are currently many cruise ships sailing around Asia. One act I know relocated his family to Thailand so he was closer to the work, saving the cruise lines $1000s in flights. As a consequence he's booked solid for seven months. Imagine the possibilities. Like Miss Mazeppa in Gypsy, "You've gotta get a gimmick."

Be patient

Once you've got everything in place - good patter, great photos, tried and tested arrangements, and you've got a fantastic showreel to prove it - be prepared to wait. Even with a personal recommendation and an agent who appreciates you, it's unlikely you'll get work straightaway. It can happen, but more often than not, your big chance will come when something goes wrong and a booker is in a bind. If an artiste falls ill, has a personal emergency or just gets a better offer, the pressure's on to find a last minute replacement. That's what happened to Maria King who went from a rehearsal pianist to headliner:

> When I left college, it was difficult to get work straight away. After working as an accompanist I managed to get a classical solo repertoire together for cruise ships.
>
> I found an agent but it still took over a year to get my first gig, and I think that was only because someone was ill and they were completely desperate! Two days after the call I was on my first cruise ship. I was only playing the classical sets at this stage but people started telling me, "You're great on stage, you're quite entertaining when you talk to the audience, why don't you do your own show in the theatre?" So I went to watch every single show I could. I learned a lot just from watching other entertainers. Most of the acts I saw were amazing and quite inspirational.
>
> I slowly started buying musical arrangements and eventually one cruise director gave me a chance to do my theatre show with a trio. That was great for me and slowly I got experience playing with a small band. That's how I gradually learned my repertoire for a show.
>
> I had one of my new shows filmed and sent it to my agent. It took him six months to even look at my DVD, then he rang me and said, "You're fabulous! You should be doing your own cabaret!" and I said, "I know, that's what I've been trying to tell you!" But even that wasn't enough. I was included in a showcase for

cruise ship bookers. This is where dozens of acts get 10 minutes each with a live band to show the bookers what they can do. I was so nervous but it went well.

Since then, I've been pretty busy. It took about three years from starting out to getting work as a headliner, but it was worth it.

Don't get complacent

Having representation doesn't mean you can relax all together. It's a mistake to think that you can rely entirely on your agent to fill your diary. The busiest and most successful acts I know never stop hustling to find work for themselves. They're always developing relationships with bookers and on the look out for new opportunities. For some acts, their agent is more of a business manager than a booker.

"A lot of show business, as you know, is about all the contacts you make and who you know." Denise Crosby

Joan Rivers has been at the top of her game for decades (as she once said, "It's not who you know, it's whom.") Does she rest on her laurels polishing her trophies? Not for a second. She never stops working because she never stops looking for work. As she says, "I'd advertise adult diapers if they asked me." Her agent understands her logic. "You can't get hit by lightning if you're not standing out in the rain," he says, "and nobody can stand in the rain longer than Joan Rivers. She'll just stay there and let it rain, let it rain, let it rain, because she knows lightning can hit. She knows because it's hit her more than once before. But she also knows, she has to stay out in the rain."

See your agent as a partner. You are both working towards the same goal. As Jo Martin said, never try and hide work from them by doing 'a bit on the side' to avoid paying their commission. I hear acts moaning about paying their agents all the time, but they should remember, the more money they earn from you, the more motivated they'll be to work for you.

Some dos and don'ts

Once you find an agent you're happy with, here are some dos and don'ts to bear in mind:

- Do send them your availability regularly, perhaps every week.
- Do not change your mind and say you're unavailable if the agent comes back to you with a booking. Providing no one has moved the goal posts (less money than agreed, impractical itinerary etc.), it should be a given you will accept the work.
- Do not cancel or change bookings once they are agreed.
- Do return their calls and emails promptly.
- Do not abuse privileges. If you are allowed to take a guest with you onto a ship, make sure you put the request in early enough and you don't change the details once submitted. No one wants the extra paperwork.
- Do try to be low maintenance. We artistes can be a needy, emotional lot. Try not to bother your agent unless it's necessary. If you're always on the phone whining about this or that, they'll soon get sick of you and use another act. Keith Maynard told me, "I'd rather have an act who is solid, personable and happy to be seen around the guests, than someone who loves themselves."
- Do follow the rules and behave. Have fun, but make sure you do a professional job. If you've had too much to drink, you're late for rehearsals or you're not dressed properly in front of guests, you might struggle to get rebooked. Be humble, courteous and respectful to everyone.

Remember, it's a buyers' market and there will always be someone else waiting in the wings to take your place.

Summary

To cut through the competition you need to get a gimmick, a personal recommendation and a well worded email. Most of all, you need an attention grabbing showreel. Once you find an agent, behave yourself. You might have the voice of an angel but talent will only get you so far. Remember:

- Be organised
- Be punctual
- Keep your agent updated with your availability
- Always act respectfully and professionally
- Try to be low maintenance
- Treat everyone with respect
- Try to get personal a recommendation

If you're anxious to hit the big time, Artistic Director, Ruth Leon, urges patience, "I strongly suggest singers don't even consider approaching the top venues until they have paid their dues. There are lots of clubs where singers can learn their craft. Don't be impatient. It takes a long time and a lot of heartache to be ready."

If it seems to be taking too long for the work to start coming in, don't panic. Martha Reeves said, "There are times in show business when you work so much you think you will pop your cork, and then suddenly you can't find any work." Usually, something will come in eventually. A musician once told me he never looks forward in his diary, he always looks back. Looking forward at empty pages always depressed him, but looking back he could see that in the end, he always ended up with plenty of work.

Natural talent with level-headed professionalism is a killer combination. Follow my advice and with luck, you'll never be out of work for long.

Secret 15: The Best Piece of Travel Advice, Ever

If you are lucky enough to get plenty of work, the chances are you'll be flying a lot. Here's a piece of advice that's guaranteed to help you lose weight, improve your sex life and make you look ten years younger. Well maybe it's not that good, but I promise it will make this book worth every penny. Here it is:

Only travel with hand luggage and never check a bag.

I know it's simple, but I can hardly think of another piece of advice with such huge benefits.

Save time

Check in online with no bags and you can turn up at the airport thirty to ninety minutes before your flight. When you get to the airport you skip the lines at check-in and head straight for security. Better still, when you get off your flight you save another twenty minutes by avoiding the wait at the carousel.

In 'Up In The Air', George Clooney tells his protégé that most people spend around thirty-five minutes waiting at check-in lines, which given how often he flies, adds up to one whole week a year. That's time worth having.

No lost luggage

Trusting an airline not to lose your luggage is like trusting a monkey not to eat a bag of complimentary peanuts.

Before I travelled 'self-contained' I reckon my bags went missing two or three times a year. As everything I needed to do my job was in those bags, I was pretty much screwed until we were reunited. That's a challenge at the best of times, but when you're sailing on a ship that's in a different country everyday… well, good luck!

If you're working on ships your contract may require you to perform even if your bags don't show up. If they go missing, you could be sent home in breach of contract.

How do you get it all in?

People are always surprised how much it's possible to squeeze into your hand luggage. Obviously you'll be wearing your clothes more than once, washing your underwear every few days and doing without your Ascot hat collection. But think though how many times you return home to unpack a pile of clothes you never even wore. Economical packing is easier than you think.

The airline industry is always changing their rules, but as I wrote this, most of them will accept two bags as carry-on: a small 'roller' case and a 'personal item' like a handbag, laptop case or backpack. My backpack is probably twice as big as what they mean by 'personal'. It's not huge, but it is substantial.

The other rule I bend is on weight. Most (though not all) airlines have a weight limit for hand luggage. With all the sheet music I have to carry, my roller is usually around 16 kgs - probably around twice the allowed weight. If you check-in online you can bypass the staff at the desk and go straight to the departure gate, which means no one's going to check the weight of your bags.

My packing list

So I don't forget anything, and because I love a list, I use one to help me pack. Here's what I get into my carry-on bags:

- Two suits
- Four formal shirts
- One pair of formal shoes
- Underwear
- Trainers and gym gear
- Swimwear
- Shorts
- Jeans
- Four T-shirts
- Flip-flops
- Toiletries
- Laundry detergent
- Sunblock
- Worldwide adaptor plug
- e-Book reader
- Camera
- iPad
- Music for two full shows with an eight piece band
- CDs to sell

Tips

All I need for four different 'outfits' is four different ties against a white shirt and black suit. My black suit is the right cut to be worn as a tuxedo with a dress shirt, cummerbund and bow tie.

I have the shoes I travel in and pack one pair of formal (black patent) shoes, trainers for the gym and flip-flops.

If it's bulky - wear it. If I am going somewhere cold I'll travel in a good coat, sweater and walking boots.

When it comes to toiletries, you're limited on the liquids you can check. You can easily decant small amounts of sunscreen, laundry detergent and moisturiser into small, carry-on friendly, plastic containers. Use a solid deodorant, small tube of toothpaste, and the shampoo provided free in your room (or better still, shave your head, like I did). Worse case: buy what you need when you arrive.

Sexual equality

When I share all this with my girl friends, they laugh and tell me they need two carry-on bags just for their make-up. They always say, "Oh, it's easy for men! Women need lots of shoes, bags and outfits." Really? Embrace black as your new best friend and your bags will be 10 kgs lighter. A couple of black dresses, one pair of black shoes and plenty of accessories will give you loads of options for a week away.

Hang on, did I just give fashion advice to women? I believe I did, and I'm sorry. But here's some more…

If you're away for longer than a week you'll just have to accept that you'll be wearing the same outfits more than once. You might hear sharp intakes of breath as you enter a room, other ladies may be shocked and appalled as they peak over fluttering fans, but you'll survive.

I've been doing this for about eight years and have never once been pointed at for wearing the same tie two nights running. For that matter, no airport staff has ever challenged me on the size, weight or number of my bags.

Seriously, it is quite possible to travel light but if you really can't manage without a whole different outfit every night, it's up to you to balance to benefit of choices against the risk of the airline loosing your bags. If you must check a bag make sure you keep the basics stuff you need for your show in your carry on. Use the checked bag for everything else.

In a typical year I will take over seventy flights. I never check a bag. I reckon I save myself about eleven working days of time. Is that worth wearing the same pair of shoes every night? You bet.

Get a watch

While we're on the subject, here's another piece of travel advice you think you don't need. Get a watch, and use it.

Every day I spend in port, scuba diving in Australia or skydiving in Africa, is marred by the constant, nagging fear that I'll miss the ship. João Wolf told me:

> If you are late for the ship it can be a big problem. It's terrible for everyone because we need to land the person's passport and they'll have to pay for their own ticket to get to the next port. He or she better have a very good excuse, backed up with a police or medical report of some kind, otherwise they may well be sent home.

A Brazilian friend of mine recently married an English girl. On the wedding day he arranged to meet the father of the bride at ten o'clock. He had a lot on his mind, but anxious to make a good impression he arrived fifteen minutes early. The father, however, turned up twenty-five minutes late. My friend was not impressed. "I thought you said 10 o'clock!" he shouted at the father. "No," he calmly replied, "I said 10 ish." My friend stared at him, "Ish?! What the hell's 'ish'?" He speaks good English, but he'd never heard of "ish" before. He's not alone. There is not a single cruise ship captain in the world who is familiar with "ish". If they say ten o'clock, they mean it.

Once, in Barbados, a guest left her husband on board and took her two kids out for the day with one of the ship's staff. Neither realised the ship was scheduled to leave early that day and no one thought to check. They returned to the quayside at 3.30pm but the ship had already gone. Worse still, it was crossing the Atlantic, so the next port of call was four days away. With the husband fretting on board, they had no choice but to fly to the

Azures and meet the ship there. Due to bad weather though, the captain couldn't dock in the Azures and had go straight to Southampton. More flights, at their expense, and the party of four finally met the ship in Southampton. Not the vacation they were expecting!

The other thing João says is:

> Read your paperwork. Sometimes acts try to come on board without the proper paperwork, medicals or visas. It's the artiste's responsibility to check all this. You can say, 'Oh, my agent never told me,' but at the end of the day you'll be the one without a job.

Once, keen to make the most of my day in New York, I left it a little late to get to the ship. I got a cab from Times Square to the cruise terminal in Brooklyn, about 45 minutes away. No ship. I panicked. I'd always joined the ship in Brooklyn before. I checked my paperwork to find that this time the ship was in Manhattan, another 45 minutes back to where I'd started. I should have been on the ship by 2pm and it was now 3.30pm. Sweating and red-faced, I finally arrived as they were about to sail. An unforgettable reminder to allow plenty of time, read my paperwork and check my watch.

Secret 16: Simon Cowell Is Not Your Friend

Cruise ships are a great place for many cabaret artistes to work but are they right for you?

Amongst the genuine talent in every year's 'X' Factor, the usual batch of hopeless hopefuls is paraded around for our guilty pleasure. Despite their various failings, I pity the contestant that should prompt Simon Cowell's now annual criticism of being "too cabaret" or "too cruise ship".

Using cruise ships as a term of abuse is par for the course for Cowell, but what's he basing his opinions on? Has he been on a cruise recently? Does he know, for example, that Rihanna's worked on one? How about Tony Bennett? Would he call James Taylor too cruise ship? They've all done it. Perhaps he'd be interested to know that Chicago is currently wowing audiences in a 1380 seat, state of the art theatre at sea. Too "cruise ship" for Mr Cowell?

We should remember that we're talking about the man who introduced the British public to a Michael Jackson impersonator dressed as Darth Vader and the fleeting joys of Jedward. Two acts unlikely to be invited to grace the stage of any ship I know.

So what does Cowell mean when he says, "too cruise ship"? Tired lounge acts churning out wallpaper music? Maybe he saw Frasier Crane's encounter with The Barracuda and thinks all cruise ship acts are washed up has-beens who spend more time working on their tans than their acts. Or maybe he cringed at the stale cruise director in 'Out To Sea' with an act cheesier than a fondue party. Well, yes, you might find a bit of that lingering in the recesses of some ships where the carpets are as old as the jokes, but it's far from representative. Things have come a long way since the Love Boat.

What makes cruise ships different

Cruise entertainment presents some unique challenges. Audiences can be very mixed: young families on a budget, retired executives and people from all parts of the globe with their own cultural references and languages - each with their own idea of what constitutes good entertainment. With such a wide degree of tastes and expectations it's often necessary to appeal to as many people as possible by presenting a 'safe' selection of inoffensive comedy, music and dance. Anything too specific risks alienating sections of the audience. Larger ships solve this by offering something for everyone in multiple venues. Choice is paramount and it's easy to forget you're on a ship at all. Celebrity's Solstice class, for example, offers seven completely different entertainment venues. On any evening you could enjoy a classical recital, contemporary jazz, or a Cirque de Soleil style production show. It's up to you.

Jeff Harnar's one singer who's learned to adapt his show without losing integrity:

> While I'd welcome any New York audience to see my cruise ship shows, I do try to make my repertoire on the high seas as accessible as possible. That said, even if I am veering to more familiar standards, I try to program them with the same integrity as I would for a New York cabaret room.
>
> I'm mindful that on land my audience has chosen to

attend and paid a fee - on the ships, we entertainers are more like another buffet - they can take what they like and leave the rest. It's helpful to have a varied menu that will appeal to most guests.

Many lines have been successful in segmenting the market to focus on one particular demographic. SAGA Cruises are exclusive to the over-50s, Royal Caribbean markets itself to adventure-seeking families and Cunard attracts those looking for traditional quality and elegance.

Talent competitions like Cowell's are in part responsible for the demise of quality light entertainment on television. As musical director Barry Robinson told me:

> I believe stage craft is something learned by experience and by physically being in many varied musical situations. It's what used to be called 'paying your dues' and it's why I have a major problem with talent shows that seem to monopolise our television screens. Standing in a queue, hoping for a shot at fame, is not a fast-track to developing stagecraft. This is why most so-called 'stars' disappear as quickly as they're discovered.

Are you a good fit for cruise ships?

Regardless of Simon Cowell's prejudice, to do well on ships requires a certain type of personality. You have to be approachable and happy to mix with people. As Keith Maynard says "You can't just get in your car and drive home at the end of the night. You're on a ship. You'll be eating alongside the same people every day of your contract."

Some cruise lines are really keen for entertainers to mix with the guests and may even ask you to host tables in the dining room. Royal Caribbean's Director of Entertainment, Ken Rush, told me that for him, it doesn't really mind either way. "If you're happy to hang out with guests," he says, "it's an added bonus" so go for it. If you'll rather keep a low profile it's fine. If you're selling CDs after your show, that's a great opportunity for guests to meet you, take a photo and connect with you. Many Royal contracts are what we call "fly-ons" - you get there, do the show and leave the next day, so you're hardly on the ship. Other lines will have you there for a whole week so there is much more opportunity to mix with the guests.

Wherever you work, there are certainly pros and cons to being a solo act. Tara Khaler sums it up well:

You're always on the move and travel can be tiring. Every new venue means you have to make new friends, get to know the staff, the band and the technicians. You have to be very sociable.

When I was in a production cast it was easy to hide away and stay in my little group, now it's important to be seen out and about. If you don't enjoy chatting to people you will struggle. On the other hand, it's a lot more gratifying to perform your own show. Maria King says:

> Don't think it's all easy, because it's not. A waiter once said to me, "You only work one night a week," and I said, "Well, give me a tray and we'll swap jobs!" I'm not saying being a waiter is easy, but to entertain an audience for 50 minutes takes years of graft.
>
> The travelling can be exhausting and people do get burnt out because they don't pace themselves. It can sometimes be lonely too, but the more you do, the more entertainers you meet. It is good money, but it should be - when you go on stage you have to be able to deliver. You need confidence and a thick skin.

If a new act wants to make a good impression, they should be willing to mix easily with guests. Maybe 'de-greet' after your show by standing outside the theatre doors as the audience is leaving. People like to meet the act and it's an easy way to make a good impression with the guests and the cruise director.

I know some entertainers who spend their time onboard trying to ingratiate themselves with the cruise director, hoping it'll lead to more work. I've often wondered if it really makes a difference. Royal's Ken Rush told me he does like his acts to make contact once they get on the ship, just to say a quick hello and let them know you've arrived safely. Do respect how busy they are and don't be offended if they don't have time to hang out. João Wolf told me:

> The more experienced and professional the act and the better the show they have, the less they'll be trying to schmooze the cruise director. Speaking personally, we have so much on our plates, that the less we have to deal with the acts, the better. Of course, my door's always open, but if an act comes on board, does a great job and only catches me in the wings to say 'hi', it's perfect.
>
> Having said all that, if it's your first time on a ship with an unusual demographic, it's not a bad idea to ask the cruise director or production manager if there's anything you should know. Asking for a little help, without sounding insecure, will open the door to as much time as they want to give you.

If you're performing on one leg of a world cruise, where guests see different singers every few days for four months, you should ask if any of your songs have already been performed. There's only so many times anyone can listen to Time To Say

Goodbye or My Heart Will Go On and My Way.

Here are Keith Maynard's tips for working on a ship:

- Be yourself.
- Be open.
- Spend the first few days observing your audience.
- Be prepared to change your act to suit the audience.
- Be punctual.
- Check any paperwork you're given straightaway - you may need to film a TV show or attend a rehearsal an hour later.
- Enjoy yourself.

Most of all though, Keith says, "Sincerity is the key. Whatever you do, you have to be seen to be sincere and genuine."

If you have problems on board, speak to your immediate superior first. In most cases this will be the production manager. Don't go straight to the cruise director or hotel manager - they have enough on their plate. If it's necessary your production manager will take it up the chain of command.

Be careful not to get a bad reputation. Alarm bells will ring if an act switches agents every five minutes. Booking agents, though competitors, will often share information on artistes that are likely to cause problems.

Be prepared to take the rough with the smooth. Logistics, for example, can sometimes be a source of frustration. As Gary Parkes says:

> These days no one has the time to micro manage travel arrangements. Saving money is always at the forefront of a booker's mind and the cheapest flights may not be ideal for the artiste.

I once left home at 4 am, took a succession of taxis, trains and planes to finally arrive at a cruise ship half way across the world over 30 hours later. Exhausted and jet lagged, I was greeted by an apologetic cruise director, "Sorry, you'll have to rest later. Your show's tonight and you have rehearsal in twenty minutes." Sometimes it's tough, but despite what your ego's saying, it's not all about you. Cruise directors are juggling a lot of elements to give the guests the best experience possible. When faced with a challenge like that, all you can do is get on with it and do the best job you can. Your professionalism won't go unnoticed.

For me, the actual show is the easiest part of my work - the hard bit is travelling to and from gigs. As Tony Bennett said, "We get paid for the travelling, not the singing."

Opportunities for new acts of real substance to develop a national profile are few and far between. The British social club scene has all but disappeared and without a 'name' topping the bill, theatre is a huge gamble. Cruise ships are one of the few places where skilled entertainers of real substance can ply their trade and make a good living.

When Simon Cowell criticises his contestants for being "too cruise ship" he's denigrating a huge industry that's giving valuable work to literally thousands of performers.

Conclusion

At the beginning of this book I promised to show you how to produce your own show, travel the world and get paid to do what you love. I hope I've lived up to that promise.

I've learned a lot writing it, especially from my friends and colleagues who were generous enough to share their own secrets in these pages. I am so grateful to them.

Critic Lisa Martland told me why she thinks cabaret is such a special art-form and shared some valuable advice for anyone new to the profession:

> I fell in love with the art of cabaret when, as a young girl, I was taken to see Steve Ross perform at the Ritz Hotel in London. For me, he still remains the personification of all that is wonderful about cabaret. He takes that risk of being on a stage with just his voice, personality, piano and spotlight for company. No sets or props to rely on, just his talent and a special way of interpreting the popular song.
>
> Musical theatre is special because of the way songs work within a libretto, allowing the audience to be part of the drama, to experience the highs and lows of emotion. Within a cabaret, an artiste might choose a composition originally written for a Cole Porter, Rodgers and Hammerstein, Sondheim show etc, but he or she will then go on to discover a fresh emotion in the

lyrics/melody and one which resonates with every member of the audience present. This quality allows an individual to engage with an artiste in a way no other art-form offers.

The other pleasure in seeing performers like Steve Ross is witnessing the joy they derive from the music they choose and the way their knowledge of the compositions is so cleverly immersed in their chat to the audience. And just as musical theatre can lead one to cabaret, so cabaret can encourage you to check out a previously unknown composer or show.

Most importantly of all, I would advise performers who are considering putting together a cabaret to remember it is an art-form in its own right. That there is so much more to it than just standing in a small room singing a string of songs that the artistes likes and he/she thinks the audience will like to.

The best cabaret performers carefully shape their shows around the material they have chosen and the anecdotes/chat/banter they are going to include in-between the numbers. Go see other performers for inspiration about what to do and not do, and listen/watch the likes of Nancy LaMott or Julie Wilson in action – YouTube is only a click away.

The material you choose and the way you shape that into a performance that the audience will engage with – laugh, cry etc. – is vital. In addition, if an artiste is afraid of revealing something personal about themselves, of opening up a little of themselves to the audience and inviting them to join them on a musical journey, then ultimately, the audience might have been entertained, but they won't have been present at the best kind of cabaret.

Fellow critic, Mark Shenton, advises anyone starting out to:

> Build your social media profile urgently - that's where you'll find audiences. Support your fellow artists and immerse yourself in the greats. Listen to Barbara Cook and the late Margaret Whiting. Feel free to borrow some of their techniques, but also make it your own; there's no point copying. Choose great material. But don't just do obvious stuff - do we really need to hear your 'Over the Rainbow'?
>
> I would also hold up Ann Hampton Callaway, my personal cabaret goddess, as a shining example in how to 'own' a room with personality, music and choices; she's warm, funny and musical. I love her sister Liz, too, for the same reasons - together, they're cabaret heaven. And of course the unofficial custodian of all things cabaret and the great American songbook is Michael Feinstein, who again has an effortless ease; there's no place he'd rather be, so there's no place you'd rather be, either. Seeing him is always a musical education; he sets every song in context, and has a story for every occasion. In the UK, there's no one quite like Barb Jungr - a jazz-based cabaret singer who has a musical intelligence that is second to none.

For this handful of cabaret stars there are thousands more struggling to get by. Eleanor Keenan thinks it's good to be prepared, "It can be a tough business and no matter how good you are, you won't always be in work. My advice to anyone starting out now is be nice and don't put all your eggs in one basket."

"Performing is all about communication." Barbara Dickson

Barbara Dickson is equally accomplished as a singer and an actress. I asked her how useful her acting skills have been in her singing career. "Performing is all about communication. When 'storytelling' is at its best, there is acting involved in the music, but I don't think singing and acting are the same as most singers can't act or vice versa." Her top tip is simply, "Keep your head up so everyone can see your face and you can be heard."

Producer Clive Thomas says, "If you want to work with us, research what we do. Invite me to a gig and be realistic about fees. I want someone who chats to the audience as well as he sings, otherwise it's just like watching an audition."

Corporate audiences can be very different to those in theatre where people buy a ticket for the kind of shows they like. Away from the disciplines and conventions of a theatre or cabaret room, corporate crowds can be rowdy, boozy and have short attention spans - a real challenge for any singer. As Clive says, "Our singers need to understand that only a part of the evening is about them. They have to be flexible when things run late, be prepared to change their sets and not act like a diva!"

> *"Be unique. Be a storyteller. And don't take yourself too seriously." Liz Callaway*

He's right, no one can be bothered with diva attitudes these days. When the work and plaudits start rolling in, remember these wise words from Robert Blair, over 200 years ago:

> When self-esteem or others' adulation,
> Would cunningly persuade us we are something,
> Above the common level of our kind,
> The grave gainsays the smooth complexioned flattery,
> And with the blunt truth acquaints us to what we are.

I keep trying to be a diva but no one takes any notice. On one ship recently I was allowed to use the backstage launderette. I finished my performance, and as the band played and the lights flashed, 800 people got to their feet, applauding and cheering for more. I left the stage, waving and smiling and walked straight to the tumble dryer to see if my socks were dry. I think that's the kind of "blunt truth" Robert Blair was talking about.

Be a specialist
A lot of people want this job. To increase your chances of being noticed it pays to specialise. I used to sing a bit of everything in my shows - musical theatre, rock 'n' roll, swing, pop and so on. I was just another reliable all-rounder in an already crowded marketplace. After my stint in the 'Rat Pack' I decided to market myself as more of an expert in one genre. I put my Motown Medley away in favour of Frank Sinatra and Dean Martin. Rather than being a jack-of-all-trades (and master of none) I became recognised as a specialist.

John Wilson agrees with that approach:

The best piece of advice I was ever given? 'The road to hell is paved with versatile people'. Someone told me that when I was 24 and it helped me to focus on the one thing I was best at, instead of trying to do lots of things reasonably well.

If they tell you it's impossible, ignore them
Whether it's Las Vegas, Marmite or the wind-up radio, it's easy to see something that's already successful and say, "Well, that was always going to happen. It was fate," but I'm not sure I believe in fate. Fate is what some people use to make sense of bad luck, or excuse their laziness. I believe in hard work, focus and determination.

The fact is, the hundreds of household names we all take for granted almost never made it past the drawing board. They only exist because of happy accidents and unhealthy obsessions. Some people are so convinced they have a great idea, they ignore years of rejection and make it happen anyway. These are my heroes. They inspire me to be the best I can be and to carry on, regardless of the naysayers.

Trevor Baylis, inventor of the wind-up radio, worked tirelessly on his revolutionary idea. He invested every penny, re-mortgaged his home, and neglected his family and friends. For years every banker, investor and marketeer slammed the door in his face. The 'experts' wrote him off as a crank. Seven years later, he was awarded the OBE and won the World Vision Award for Development Initiative. His inventions have since changed the lives of millions and Trevor Baylis is a household name.

Michael Bublé has sold more than 30 million albums worldwide. Hailed by the critics (mostly) and public alike, he's considered by many to be at the top of his game. With that voice and stage presence, it's easy to think his stardom was inevitable. Nothing could be further from the truth.

After spending much of his youth working with his dad's commercial fishing crew, at 16 he got his first professional singing engagement. The next seven years was spent schlepping around every gig he could find: shopping malls, lounges, weddings and yes, cruise ships. Was everyone hailing the birth of star? Were agents clamouring to sign him up? Nope. By the time he was twenty-five his dreams of stardom were fading. Just as he was thinking about giving up, his luck began to change.

An aide to former Canadian Prime Minister, Brian Mulroney, showed Bublé's self-financed album to his boss. He liked it and hired Bublé to sing at their daughter's wedding. As it happened, multi Grammy Award winning producer and record executive David Foster was one of the guests. If you don't know Foster, you will know some of the people he's worked with: Madonna, Josh Groban, Whitney Houston, Michael Jackson, Céline Dion, Barbra Streisand and Andrea Bocelli. Foster liked Bublé but was reluctant to sign him because he, "Didn't know how to market this kind of music."

Undeterred, Bublé seized the initiative. Taking his agent along for support, he moved to Los Angeles with the sole purpose of persuading Foster to sign him. Eventually he got the news he was waiting for. Yes, Foster would produce an album, but Bublé had to find the $500,000 to pay for it. The money was found (in the end Foster covered the bill) and he was on his way.

Of course, Bublé has great talent, but so do lots of people. Talent alone is no guarantee of stardom. Bublé says he always knew exactly what he wanted to be. He worked hard and when his chance came he grabbed it with both hands.

"Big shots are only little shots who keep on shooting."
Christopher Morley

He couldn't have predicted meeting David Foster, but by taking every gig that came along, making his own album, and always doing his best, he upped the odds of something good happening. Was it just luck? I don't thing so. Luck, fate, whatever you want to call it, does play a big part, but so does hard work and application. As Frank Sinatra said:

> People often remark that I'm pretty lucky. Luck is only important in so far as getting the chance to sell yourself at the right moment. After that, you've got to have talent and know how to use it.

Get used to rejection

After a fleeting television appearance in February 1995, I sent a brochure and promotional tape to exactly one-thousand entertainment agents. Six months later, the total number of respondents was precisely zero. Only on Boxing Day of that year did someone call me. That single call led to my West End break and my own UK tour.

This modest success is inconsequential in the great scheme of things, but it was a good lesson learned. I had nine-hundred and ninety-nine nos and one yes - that's a success rate of 0.1%. Not great odds, but it was enough.

As a performer you'll have to get used to being judged and being rejected. Bookers aren't just sitting there waiting to hear from you. It takes time and patience to sell anything new. Expect to hear "No thank you", and "We're still not interested", and "Please stop calling us" but don't let any of it put you off.

"A man is a success if he gets up in the morning and gets to bed at night, and in between he does what he wants to do." Bob Dylan

I have many friends who spend their lives trudging from one audition to another only to be sent away because they're too young, too old, too fat or too thin. Growing a skin thick enough to leave their self-confidence intact takes some serious self-belief. Eventually, with talent and perseverance, they might get their lucky break. In the meantime, they never give up - constantly improving and performing whenever they can. This is why you need to love what you do. Only those truly passionate about performing will stay the course. They're not doing it for fame and money. For them, there's as much pleasure in the journey as there is in the destination.

Lisa Leob said, "My overnight success was really 15 years in the making. I'd been writing songs since I was 6 and playing in bands since I was 14."

Success is rarely a single, life changing event. It's a hundred simple habits, repeated every day.

How do we cope with career set backs and disappointments?

We artists love to create. We get inspired and we go to work. Our latest project is always the most exciting and it's easy to assume that everyone will agree that our newest album, show, song, or whatever, is just what the world's been waiting for. That is, until we share our new masterpiece with the world and other than a few likes on Facebook, nothing much happens and the world moves swiftly onto the next new, shiny thing.

The number of artists (be they painters, singers, dancers or whatever) who actually break through and achieve fame and success is so tiny that I think it's a matter of self-preservation to be stoical about our work. We should set realistic goals and create work that we're passionate about and not because we think it's what we should be doing.

Let's say I write a song with the primary aim of pleasing a particular audience. I make loads of compromises, I don't really like the result myself, but I'm sure it will tick the necessary boxes to be a success. It's released and nobody really likes it. It's a big, fat failure.

On the other hand, if I release a song that I feel passionately about, that comes from the heart, I will feel it's a success regardless of how many Likes it gets and how often it's downloaded. I will have created art for myself first, and that has to be what counts. If not, we're forever chasing the latest trend and losing our artistic integrity along the way.

Of course, we want our work to be seen and heard, but if our measure of success is getting a number record or being shown in the National Gallery, statistically, we will probably end up disappointed.

I'm not famous, but I don't consider myself a failure. I am still enthusiastic about my career because just by making my living doing what I love, I've achieved more than I dared to hope. Any more would just be icing on the cake.

Let's simply aim to realise our own potential and to make the most of the talent we've been given. Yes, let's be ambitious but at the same time, keep it real. For it is in unrealistic expectations that the seeds of disappointment and the bitterness are born.

Work hard and be prepared

Michael Feinstein says there's no substitute for practise and practical experience. He told me:

> You can study forever, but to really learn your craft, you have to be in front of an audience - any audience, and all kinds of audiences. I would often sing in retirement homes - they were grateful for entertainment and I learned a lot in the process.
>
> There are always places where people would be grateful for some music. Find a neighbourhood hang out and sing there. If you can get a regular or weekly gig, then people can come back to hear you again. While the Internet is fantastic, it is only hands-on experience that will properly prepare you for the stage when your big chance arrives.

Jeff Harnar seconds that:

> My suggestion is to see as much cabaret as you can. Find what resonates with you and how others navigate the art form. I try to say yes to as many opportunities as possible.
>
> Whether for a benefit, a local church or open mic, I'm always happy to sing for free where my music can be of service. There's a seasoning that comes from being in front of audiences as frequently as possible that can't be manufactured or learned in any other way. I also

listen to all feedback and read my reviews to know if there are any recurring observations on what's working and what's not. In order to be successful commercially, I must be rigorously honest with myself about how my work is being received.

Hard work, it seems, is a prerequisite to success. Founder of the London Cabaret Awards, Paul L. Martin says to anyone entering the world of cabaret:

> Do as many open slots as you can. Meet as many performers, promoters and venue owners as you can. Learn from other acts and audiences. Don't assume this will be easy or instant. It will take you years of traipsing about singing for nothing (or a glass of wine) before something clicks and you find your voice and earn your stripes. Oh, and be nice to the sound man – he has the power to turn off your mic!

Kim Gavin thinks there's little substitute for hard work:

> The worst thing I see is people not pushing themselves enough. You've got to feel as though you've given it every shot to be the best you can be. I'm not a big fan of the 'X' Factor in the UK, but I will say that it's the best school of all time. The contestants know that if they want to be there next week, they have to get better. If they don't, they're out. So don't get complacent and never give up. Keep working hard to be the best singer you can and understand it takes more than that to be a star.

Sue Raney has worked with Billy May, Henry Mancini and

Dean Martin to name a few. Julie Andrews said of her, "she is a marvel". I was lucky enough to work with Sue and the Nelson Riddle Orchestra a few years ago and her advice to anyone starting out is:

> Keep your voice in shape by doing all the proper exercises to retain it. That gives you the confidence you need to know your instrument is going to be in the best form. Always know your songs so well that you can relax and have fun with the audience. Remember you're a performer while you sing, but the audience must see the person behind the voice, so they can enjoy not only your expertise, but also your warmth.

Andrea Marcovicci's told me her best cabaret advice is "Listen to Mabel Mercer and make the lyric the most important thing." I like that. It reminds me of Frank Sinatra when he said, "Throughout my career, if I have done anything, I have paid attention to every note and every word I sing."

I hope that the secrets I've shared with you here have given you the tools to make your dreams come true. The biggest lesson I want to share with you today is simply this: do what you love. Most people go through their lives without ever knowing what they want to do with themselves. If you've found your passion, you're one of the lucky few. If that passion is music and performing, you're even luckier. Go for it. Give it everything you've got. Enjoy every moment so that even if you don't sell 30 million albums, you'll have a hell of a time trying.

Let me leave you with this from David Ackert in the L.A. Times:

> Singers and Musicians are some of the most driven, courageous people on the face of the earth. They deal

with more day-to-day rejection in one year than most people do in a lifetime.

Every day, they face the financial challenge of living a freelance lifestyle, the disrespect of people who think they should get real jobs, and their own fear that they'll never work again.

Every day, they have to ignore the possibility that the vision they have dedicated their lives to is a pipe dream.

With every note, they stretch themselves, emotionally and physically, risking criticism and judgment.

With every passing year, many of them watch as the other people their age achieve the predictable milestones of normal life - the car, the family, the house, the nest egg.

Why? Because musicians and singers are willing to give their entire lives to a moment - to that melody, that lyric, that chord, or that interpretation that will stir the audience's soul.

Singers and Musicians are beings who have tasted life's nectar in that crystal moment when they poured out their creative spirit and touched another's heart. In that instant, they were as close to magic, God, and perfection as anyone could ever be. And in their own hearts, they know that to dedicate oneself to that moment is worth a thousand lifetimes.

Glossary

There are thousands of theatrical and musical terms I could have listed here but I decided to include those that I know are used on a regular basis in most cabaret environments. You'll find more extensive lists online.

A cappella
Singing without accompaniment from the band. Some acts will close their show with an a cappella piece like 'Somewhere Over The Rainbow'. It's easy to do but sounds impressive to an audience. The other benefit is you don't have to buy an arrangement!

Accelerando
A symbol used in musical notation telling the band to gradually speed up.

Apron
The area of the stage extending beyond the proscenium. The edge of the stage which usually projects in front of the curtain. In some theatres this can be extended by building over the orchestra pit.

Arrangement
The way a piece of music has been written for the orchestra to play. An arrangement will consist of the 'parts' or individual

pieces of music for each musician in the orchestra to play. When you commission an arrangement you can make whatever requests you like. You might change the key, add a colla voce verse, or join a few songs together to make a medley. The arrangement can have a huge effect on how a song sounds - look how the Postmodern Jukebox give contemporary songs a totally different feel.

Backdrop or backcloth
A painted canvas or plain surface upon which light can be thrown. Usually a stardrop, black or white cloth.

Backstage
The entire area behind or beyond the stage, including the dressing rooms. Sometimes includes the 'wings', or sides of the stage area.

Blocking
The process of determining where you will be on stage for each part of your show. Sometimes called 'plotting'. To help the lighting engineer, it's important to be consistent with your blocking. For example, you might always start a particular song at the stool then walk down stage towards the end, you might always walk in the house for the first chorus of another song, or stand by the piano for a particular ballad.

When I rehearse my show with the band I always walk through my blocking. This helps me get acquainted with the stage and shows the lighting engineer where I will be moving during the show.

Boom
In this sense boom refers to the adjustable piece of metal on a microphone stand. Typically you'll have the base, the main vertical pole and the boom, which can be adjusted to the desired

angle. I like to be close to the microphone, so always ask for a round-bottom stand with no boom - just a straight pole.

Build
A lighting term meaning the gradual increasing of brightness. For example the brightness during a song might build from 50% to full by the end. You might just ask the lighting engineer to add a couple of builds in a particular song.

Business
Also known as 'shtick', business refers to a routine, often involving comedy. So I might use my 'sing-along business' or 'romance business'.

Busker
Not a street performer, but a piece of music the band plays from memory, without the aid of sheet music. In America this is called a 'faked' tune, as in "Can you guys fake Blue Moon in 'C'?" There is a large repertoire of standards that most jazz based musicians will be able to busk.

Cans
Headphones.

Chord
A group of (typically three or more) notes sounded together, as a basis of harmony.

Colla Voce
Means 'with the voice' and tells the musicians that the singer will not be singing in tempo and they should listen to follow his phrasing. It's often used in the verses of songs with piano accompaniment before the tempo begins.

Condenser mic
A type of microphone which requires additional power to work. Condenser mics are generally used more for recording than for stage.

Cross Fade
A lighting term referring to fading some lights down while fading others up.

Cue
Most of my patter or chat is set and scripted, especially the last few words before I go into the next song. This acts as the cue for the musical director to start counting off the song. For example, before my Dean Martin Medley I say, "...the man who famously said, 'I only drink to steady my nerves, last night I got so steady I couldn't move!'" This is written on every piece of music in front of the band and the running order. Each time I rehearse the medley with the band I always give them the cue line, just as I do in the show. This helps the MD to get a feel for the timing so he can start counting the band off before I have finished the sentence. This means that as soon as I've finished, the band is playing. I hate those dead moments on stage when I have supplied the cue line but the MD is still checking his metronome.

Cue Sheet
A list of cues from which a stage manager, lighting operator or sound technician can work.

DI Box
Direct Injection box. A way of taking a sound signal straight from an instrument, such as an electric guitar, to the mixer of a sound system. The instrument is plugged into a jack socket in a small box which is connected to the mixer.

Director
The person charged with overall interpretation of a dramatic work, who conducts the rehearsals, blocks the action and assists the performers in developing their characters. Most cabaret artists learn to be their own director, but it can be extremely helpful to work with a professional director to offer guidance and clarity to your vision. It's very hard to find a director sensitive to the artiste's individuality. The whole point of cabaret is for the performer to reveal who they really are, not hide behind a character.

Downstage (DS)
The front of the stage, or that portion of the stage closest to the audience. Upstage is towards the back of the stage. Stage left and stage right are the left and right sides as you stand looking out at the audience. A piece of stage direction in an old publication of Macbeth read: "Lady Macbeth enters with candle, right upper entrance," and at the end of the scene instructed, "Lady Macbeth leaves with candle, left upper entrance."

Dynamics
Relative loudness or softness as marked in the sheet music.

False-tabs
A fake ending to a show, leading the audience to think it's over, when you actually have your encores prepared. Tabs means curtains, so a false-tabs is when we expect the curtains close… but they don't.

Falsetto
A style of male singing where, by partial use of the vocal chords, the voice is able to reach the pitch of a female.

Feedback
The unpleasant squealing noise you get when the sound from a speaker feeds into the mic and then back through the loudspeaker, creating a loop.

Flat
A basic unit of scenery consisting of a wooden frame. Usually covered with muslin or canvas and painted, it can also be covered with thin wooden veneer. It can also mean when a note is under the desired pitch.

Follow Spot
A high wattage, variable focus lighting instrument mounted so as to enable the operator to follow performers on stage with the beam of light. The beam of light can be sharpened or diffused to alter the effect of the lighting, and the spot can be enlarged or reduced to maintain a tight focus on the performer.

Fore-stage
See Apron. The small area of stage extending beyond the proscenium.

Forte
A symbol telling the musicians to play loud.

Fourth Wall
The imaginary fourth wall that would have once been removed from an enclosed set to enable the audience to see the action on stage. The term now applies to the invisible 'wall' separating the audience from the performers. Thus, the term 'breaking the fourth wall' refers to a performer speaking directly to the audience. This is rare in theatre but at the very heart of cabaret.

Fermata

A fermata is an articulation mark that allows a note or chord to be held for longer than normal.

Gaffer Tape (Gaffa Tape)

Sometimes called duct tape. A strong cloth tape with a flat finish that can be used to temporarily fix almost anything, mark the stage or hold a running order in place. Its big advantage is that, although it adheres firmly to most surfaces, it can be removed easily without causing any damage to the surface.

Gel

A thin sheet of coloured plastic (originally gelatine - hence the name) that is placed in a gel frame and inserted in a lighting unit to add colour to the beam of light.

Glissando (or Gliss)

Sliding between two notes.

Gobo

A thin metal disc that can be inserted into a lighting unit. The disc has a pattern cut into it allowing the beam of light to create effects such as flowers, a skyline etc.

Green Room

A room or space near the stage, used by actors and crew between acts or while waiting to go on.

House

Front of House (FoH). The entire theatre beyond the front of the stage. You might, for example, walk into the house for a particular piece of 'business'.

House Lights
The lights used to illuminate the house before, after or sometimes during a performance.

IMAG
Image Magnification. Used in shows when the performance is filmed and broadcast on screens. IMAG allows the audience to see more detail.

Interval
The distance in pitch between two notes.

Intonation
Being in tune with your accompaniment or other singers. If someone tells you your intonation is bad, tell them to mind their own business... then go practise your scales.

ISRC Code
An ISRC code is a unique code assigned to every piece of recorded music. Think of it as a bar code generated by an authorised agent, like a record label or mastering facility. It allows everyone involved in the writing, production and performance of each piece of music to track their sales and airplay.

Each code consists of four parts: the country of registration, the registrant (e.g. record company), the year and a unique code assigned by the record company to that track. For example, my recording of This Can't Be Love, recorded in 2007, has the ISRC code GB-RXN-07-81603.

Online digital distributors like IODA and CD Baby will not be able to distribute your music to digital music stores like iTunes and Amazon without an ISRC code.

Key signature
The flats and sharps at the beginning of each staff line indicating the key the piece is to be played in.

Lighting Plot
The lighting instructions for your show. A detailed lighting plot can include a scale drawing of the complete lighting rig. As you can see in chapter 8, I restrict my lighting plot to simple bullet points to advise the lighting engineer the general looks I want for each song.

Mac
A brand name for one of the most commonly used intelligent lights.

Mark or Spike
The place on stage in relation to the set and scenery, where a player is to deliver a particular line or commence some action. During rehearsals, actors practice 'finding their marks'.

Mastering
Almost all CDs are mastered before completion to prepare them for airplay and retail sale. If you're making an album, you'll need the help of a skilled mastering engineer to unify sound quality and levels.

With EQ, compression and gain, they can help your tracks sound great on any sound system. Some can generate ISRC codes for you and add CD text information.

Measure
The unit of measurement where the beats on the lines of the staff are divided up into two, three, four or more beats to a measure.

Modulation
To shift to another key.

Monitor
Also known as 'foldback'. A speaker used to monitor the sound. Sometimes off stage but in most cases, on stage, so the singer can hear themselves clearly over the band.

Notes
Refers to the notes delivered by the director to the cast and crew during and at the end of rehearsals to help improve the piece. You might ask another performer to watch your show and give you notes afterwards. Never give notes to anyone else unless they are invited - it's rude.

Offstage
Areas of the stage that are not part of the set.

Omnidirectional
A type of microphone which takes in sound coming from all directions. You'll usually work with a unidirectional mic, which takes sound from one direction only.

Parts
The pieces of music each musician plays. For example, the piano part, the drum part etc. All the parts make up the arrangement.

Phrase
A single line of music played or sung. A musical sentence.

Piano
Yes, the big musical instrument, but also an instruction in sheet music to play softly. Abbreviated by a "p".

Places
As in, "Places, please". The command given by the stage manager directing the actors and crew to assume their starting positions for the performance.

Platform
A raised box or rostrum used to elevate actors upstage.

Portamento
A mild glissando between two notes for an expressive effect.

Proscenium
The frame around the stage. Sometimes called the "prosc".

Rake
The slope of the stage from front to back, allowing the actors in the back to be seen more easily. From this practice come the terms 'upstage' and 'downstage'. Most theatres these days have raked seating instead of a raked stage.

Rallentando (rall) or Ritardando (rit)
Alternative words for the same thing, meaning a gradual decrease in speed. There are plenty of lively songs with a 'rit' a few bars from the end for dramatic effect.

Riser or Rostrum
A raised platform, moveable or fixed.

Rubato
A rubato is when strict tempo is temporarily abandoned and the piece slows down. Ballads often have a rubato section in the middle to accentuate the lyric, before the tempo picks up again.

Running Order
Your set list showing the songs you will sing in your show. I like to include information on where I will chat, when to play DVDs or move risers, and give the main chat cue lines so the band and technicians know exactly what's going on.

Run-Through
A type of rehearsal in which an act or the entire play is rehearsed without interruption. Usually this is done later in the rehearsal schedule, after the director has worked through blocking and characterisation with the players.

Scrim
A large piece of losely woven material that usually fills the width of the stage. If lighting is thrown on the front of a scrim, with no light behind, it becomes opaque. If lighting on the front is reduced and the scrim is lit from behind, it becomes transparent to the audience. Lighting can therefore be used to 'remove' a wall and permit the audience to see the action on the other side. I sometimes use this when I open my show. I start the first song on a high riser and just have my face lit through the scrim. It creates an interesting look.

Segue
Pronounced "seg-way". An uninterrupted transition from one piece of music to another. I like a lot of segues in my show and will often segue from one tune to another while chatting over a vamp. This adds pace and flow to the show and is preferable to stopping for a chat between every song.

Sharp
When a note is above the desired pitch.

Sight Lines
The lines of sight, from the extreme sides of the auditorium and from the rear of the balcony that determine the limit of the area on stage in which action can take place and be visible to the entire audience.

Slide
A glissando or portamento.

Sound Frequencies
I asked engineer, Paul Fawcus, for a 60 second introduction to sound frequencies. Here's what he told me, "Think of high as being the sibilance (hissing sound like "sh") of the voice or like a hi-hat. A little can add presence, too much will peel the skin from your face.

The mid range is the main part of the voice but pushing this can also make it worse! Sometimes, less is more. Other things sharing this range are saxes, trombones, piano and guitar, your engineer should EQ with care. Hi mid can make you sound nasal, low mid can make you sound boxy. The human voice, with a few exceptions, doesn't go very low. You rarely need anything beneath 150Hz and if any thing it just clouds the issue, especially on a gig.

To give you an idea of the whole sound spectrum and what, out of 40-20,000Hz the human ear should be able to detect, the boom of a kick drum is around 100Hz, 'A' that we tune to (in the UK) is 440Hz and a hi-hat sizzle is around 10,000Hz. The human voice sits right in the middle at 300Hz to 3400Hz.
All monitors and PAs are different, but with a typical system and standard vocal mic like an SM58, I'd usually start with a flat EQ, then cut everything under 150Hz and lose a little low mid 250-320hz."

Smoke Machine or Fog Machine
Useful for simulating smoke, mist and fog to reveal beams of light. If you want your lights to be seen let the stage staff use plenty of smoke.

Some singers complain that it affects their voices but I've never had any problem. As far as I know, it's harmless.

Special
An effect where lights are focussed on one specific part of the stage. You might ask for on overhead special and front of house special to be focussed at the stool while you sing a ballad. It can be more interesting that just using the follow spot.

Spike
A process of placing a 'mark' on stage for the performer to hit during the show.

Spot
As in spotlight. See Follow-Spot.

Stage Left
The left side of the stage when facing the audience.

Stage Right
The right side of the stage when facing the audience.

Starcloth, Stardrop
A black backdrop filled with small white lights to create a starry sky effect.

Strike
To disassemble a set or prop and remove it from the stage.

Tabs
Originally called 'tableaux drapes', but now used to mean any stage curtain.

Treads
Theatrical term for steps or stairs.

Tempo
The speed at which the regular pulse of a piece is repeated.

Thrust Stage
A type of stage which is surrounded on three sides by the audience. Like a fashion show catwalk. You might have a regular stage with a small thrust fitted to the front.

Unidirectional
A type of mic which takes sound from one direction only, as opposed to omnidirectional which takes in sound coming from all directions.

Upstage
Stage direction referring to the back of the stage, or that part furthest from the audience. Originated from the fact that stages were originally raked at an upward angle from the front to the back of the stage.

Vamp
A vamp is when the band plays a section of music, usually two or four bars, continuously until directed to move on. It's common to ask the band to "vamp till ready" while the singer talks.

Vaudeville
A type of show consisting of mixed specialty acts, including song, dance, acrobatics, comic skits and dramatic monologues.

Vibrato
Creating variation pitch in a note by quickly alternating between notes.

Wings
Flats or drapes placed at each side of the stage, either facing or obliquely towards the audience. To be "In the wings" means to be behind these flats, away from the audience's view. You'll usually wait in the wings before you make your stage entrance.

Work Lights
Lights sometimes used during rehearsals to light the stage while the technical crew is working or you're rehearsing with the band.

Appendix: Show Analyses

Interested to see if any patterns emerged, I looked at the live performances of four well-known singers. I analysed each show's template - the sections and the types of songs or chat they were doing - and what effect they had on the shape of the show. I found a number of consistencies, surprising given the range of artistes. I've tried to describe each section, but I recommend you find then and watch them to see for yourself.

Matt Monro - Live In Australia

Matt Monro was famed for his silky smooth voice. Most of his hits were ballads, so the challenge was to give the audience all the songs they came to hear, but include enough variation to keep a live show entertaining.

Running for almost 48 minutes, it is same kind of length you'd be expected to perform on a ship.

Opening Section
1. Lively, snappy, short opener: 'As Long As I'm Singing'
Not a very well known song, but it's short, snappy, and has a good opening sentiment all about how he loves to sing and make music.

The middle section of the song nicely introduces the

musicians. By using this song as his play-off later, it becomes the theme for his show.

2. Character song to connect: 'How Do You Do?'
Again, not a well known song, but it's a perfect ice-breaker; a way for him to introduce himself to the audience and break the 'fourth wall'. It's gentle, charming and has bags of personality. Matt walks around the audience shaking hands and making quips as he sings: "How do you do, it's nice to see, how do you do, so glad you're here, of all the places that I've been to, this is the nicest one by far..."

3. Ballad: 'What To Do?'
One of his big hits, which the audience greets with a round of applause. We've got the lively opener and the ice-breaker out of the way and now we're getting down to what the evening is really about - great ballads showing off Matt's unique voice.

4. Chat
He quickly welcomes the audience and makes a few gags about Melbourne. The jokes actually land flat, but he does set a light hearted mood. So these three songs and his 'welcome' chat make the opening section. You can see each piece is there for a specific reason. They are not just a bunch of songs and jokes, they are tools Matt uses to manipulate the audience.

Hits Section
5. Medium: 'My Kinda Girl'
In this section there is not much talking. It's about big hits and well known favourites. My Kinda Girl is a livelier arrangement than the original, which helps to give the show some pace, punctuating the ballads.

6. Ballad: 'Yesterday'

7. Medium: 'You're Nobody Till Somebody Loves You'

8. Chat
He tells a few self-depreciating gags, some in slightly bad taste, then introduces one of his biggest hits, Portrait of My Love.

9. Ballad: 'Portrait of My Love/Walk Away/Play-off'
A medley of two big hits. Walk Away has a strong dramatic ending and is instantly followed by his play-off music (As Long As I'm Singing) as he leaves the stage. We're only 20 minutes into the show and it's hard to know what happened once he was off stage. There could have been an interval or television break, he could have come straight back on or, as I think more likely, the band could have played an instrumental and given Matt a short break.

Bonding Section
10. Chat
To continue building the friendly rapport with the audience, Matt tells a few risqué jokes. By this time the audience has decided they like him which means he can afford to be a bit cheeky. Just like in life, when you meet someone for the first time you don't introduce yourself by telling rude jokes, but after twenty minutes of small talk, it might be more appropriate. Matt tells a comedy routine about 'false tabs' and working in Japan. He's clearly not a comedian but his chat is relaxed and shows he's got some personality. He sets up the next song by telling the audience he expects them to sing along.

11. Medium with audience participation: 'In The Arms of Love'
Matt sings the first half on stage, then goes into the house and embarrasses a few ladies by trying to get them to sing with him. I wouldn't recommend making anyone feel uncomfortable. Many artistes get an audience member on stage during their show and will often embarrass them for the amusement of everyone else. It can be funny, but I think you have a responsibility to make everyone feel relaxed, safe and happy.

12. Chat
More meandering chat then three jokes. In my opinion, if you're not a comedian you should avoid telling jokes and stick to anecdotes or simple links. Celine Dion, for example, is not a comedienne, she knows this and consequently her chat is pretty straight.

The Final Build
This is the "bam, Bam, BAM!" I like to use. Three strong songs to build towards the finale. No chat, just great songs to build the energy.

13. Ballad: 'From Russia With Love'

14. Up: 'Hey There Georgie Girl'
Not one of his hits, but a popular song of the day. Interestingly this is a very short version, only about ninety seconds long. I think he did this just to break up the string of ballads.

15. Ballad: 'Born Free + play-off'
One of the songs people were waiting to hear. The band plays the same 'As Long As I'm Singing' play-off but Matt doesn't

leave the stage, it's there just to send a signal to the audience that the show is almost over.

Finale Section
16. Chat
Just a short intro to the last song.

17. Dramatic ballad: 'Softly + play-off'
Softly has a great sentiment to close a show and a powerful dramatic build. We have the same 'As Long As I'm Singing' play-off for Matt to exit.

Michael Bublé - Caught In The Act

In this show Bublé is everything a terrific act should be: great voice, slick presentation and a natural charisma on stage. He completely charms the audience so they feel that it's all just for them.

Opening Section
1. Dramatic: 'Feeling Good'
The colla voce opening to this arrangement is very useful. People expect every show to open with a bang. By starting very quietly and intimately the audience is drawn in, it focusses them and builds their anticipation. When the band explodes the contrast is all the more powerful.

2. Lively: 'Sway'
He segues straight into another big hit, giving the audience what they came for. Interestingly he counts the band in himself. This isn't necessary musically (he has an MD) but suddenly everyone on stage is looking to him for direction. This gives the audience the impression that Bublé is in control leading the band, that he's the leader, the boss.

3. Chat
So after using these two big songs to introduce himself to his audience it's time to chat. It's a masterclass in how to be natural and sincere. He's funny too and the audience loves him for it.

4. Ballad: 'Try A Little Tenderness'
By sitting on a stool Bublé creates an intimate atmosphere to contrast with the opening two songs. His voice sounds great and the lyric of this suits his image as a ladies man. As the

arrangement builds he walks down-stage, which adds interest and energy.

Bonding Section
5. Medium: 'Fever'
Immediately after the ballad he counts the band in by clicking his fingers. It's a very cool segue and a good build from the last ballad. This song includes some fun participation with the band.

6. Chat
Bublé jokes about the audience taking photographs. It's all very natural and seemingly spontaneous (though as we know, it's thoroughly rehearsed).

He goes into the house and the women go crazy. Everyone gets on their feet and the band vamps ready for the next tune. It's electrifying.

7. Up: 'Come Fly With Me'

8. Up: 'Moondance'

9. Chat
He introduces some of his musicians then sits and pays homage to Ray Charles with two ballads.

10. Ballad: 'You Don't Know Me/That's All'

11. Medium: 'For Once In My Life'

12. Chat
Before introducing his special guest, Bublé asks a girl from the audience to dry his face with a towel; it's a nice moment.

Special Guest Section
This section breaks the show up, adds more interest and gives Bublé a chance to have fun with his guests.

13. Romantic ballad: 'You'll Never Find Another Love Like Mine' (with Laura Pausini)

14. Chat
Self depreciating chat and some teasing of the audience about jazz. He does an impression of Josh Groban who then joins him for a surprise duet.

15. Pop: 'This Love'
Bublé surprises everyone here by singing a pop song. It add more colour to the set and shows off his versatility.

Filler Section
It was hard to know what to call this section, three songs that don't belong anywhere else. The chat before 'Home' is very intimate and The More I See You nicely changes the mood again.

16. Medium: 'Under My Skin'
After the pop song, this great Sinatra standard gets us firmly back to the swing music that Bublé is best known for.

17. Chat
It amazing what a strong effect a small piece of stage blocking can have. By sitting on the front of the stage Bublé puts himself almost in the laps of his audience. The fourth wall is well and truly broken and the mood made very intimate. He talks about growing up listening to his favourite radio show and how he felt years later on hearing one of his own songs played on the same station. It's tender and revealing, and sets up the next song.

18. Hit song: 'Home'

19. Medium: 'More I See You'
Continues the intimate mood before building towards the finale.

Final Build Section
Here's that bang, Bang, BANG! ending again. Three very well known, up tempo songs, designed to build the energy in the room and get the audience on their feet.

20. Up: 'Save The Last Dance'

21. Up: 'How Sweet It Is To Be Loved By You'
Bublé says his goodbyes over the intro for this song, sending a signal that the show will be over soon. He leaves the stage over a play-off and the audience shouts for more. The band stops playing but they are still lit, so it's obvious that there is more to come.

22. Up: 'Crazy Little Thing Called Love'
There is no chat. As soon as Bublé walks back on stage the music starts.

Finale Section
23. Chat
Just a few final thank yous before closing with a ballad.

23. Sentimental ballad: 'A Song For You'
Like 'My Way' and 'I Will Always Love You' this is a strong, evocative ballad. It gives the audience a sincere heartfelt goodbye. Bublé leaves the stage to a slow play-off. As someone once told me, "the slower the play-off, the bigger the star."

Céline Dion - A New Day

Produced by Franco Dragone, this stylish show incorporates dancers in Cirque style costumes to fill the huge Vegas stage. Like Matt Monro, Celine Dion is best known for her ballads, so the challenge is to keep the show varied enough with different styles and tempos to keep the live audience entertained. The dramatic, and at times epic, staging helps to break up the 'sameness', always keeping the audience visually entertained.

Opening Section
1. Sentimental ballad: 'A New Day Has Come'
This is an unusual opening section in that she sings five similar songs with no chat. Opening with a gentle, romantic ballad immediately draws everyone in, it calms and focuses the audience and sets a sophisticated tone. After an intimate start the song builds to a dramatic close.

2. Dramatic ballad: 'Power Of Love'
After the intimacy of the opening song, this thrills the audience with spectacular staging.

3. Dramatic ballad: 'It's All Coming Back To Me Now'

4. Dramatic ballad: 'Because You Love Me'

5. Dramatic ballad: 'To Love You More'

6. Chat: Welcome chat
We are now seventeen minutes into the show and finally, she speaks. Her chat is pleasant and predictable. She's not funny or insightful, just polite, but what she does works perfectly well.

Energy Section

These two lively songs are necessary to break up the run of five ballads.

7. Up: 'I'm Alive'
The show gets the lift it needs with the most visually engaging set piece so far. Lots of dancers and great lighting.

8. Up: 'I Drove All Night'
A faster tempo still as the energy continues to build.

Sentimental Section
9. Intimate ballad: 'Seduces Me'
The energy is pulled back down with a theatrical and sophisticated introduction to this song.

10. Chat
There are no tabs to hide the stage as it's being cleared, so Dion has to talk here to 'fill-in'. She jokes about the set then talks about children. By sitting on the front of the stage, she adds intimacy. She dedicates the next song to her own child.

11. Intimate ballad: 'If I Could'
There is a dramatic build in this song, but it's basically heartfelt and sentimental. She helps to maintain the intimacy by sitting on the side of the stage for the whole song.

12. Chat
She chats more here to maintain the intimacy. The chat is personal and sentimental.

13. Intimate ballad: 'Pour Que Tu M'aimes Encore'

14. Dramatic ballad: 'I Surrender'

15. Medium, theatrical: 'Ammore Annascunnuto'
This piece opens with large scale, theatrical staging which gives Dion time to change and catch her breath. This is not a sentimental ballad like the other songs in the section, but it does serve to punctuate the mood.

Sinatra Section
Sinatra songs are perfect for any Vegas show and a gift for Dion as the big band mood provides a welcome change to her signature contemporary ballads.

16. Chat
Dion is not a great communicator like Bublé, so like most of her patter, this is straightforward but adequate.

17. Ballad: 'All The Way' (duet with Sinatra)
Using the screens with Sinatra singing adds another element to the show and keeps the audience visually engaged.

18. Up: 'I've Got The World On A String'
The brilliant staging and big band sound provide a refreshing change of mood.

Build Section
19. Up: 'I Wish'
Here it is again, that bang, Bang, BANG! ending. There are lots of dancers with stunning staging to build the energy and get the audience excited. To make her point, Dion even says, "Can you call 911? This is the part of the show that's crazy!" then she 'faints' on stage.

20. Up: 'Love Can Move Mountains'
The energy continues to build as she gets everyone to stand and dance. The backing vocalists take the end section of the song to give Dion a chance to leave the stage and change.

21. Up: 'River Deep, Mountain High'
Building still more with this failsafe crowd pleaser.

Finale Section
22. Dramatic ballad (hit): 'My Heart Will Go On'
This visually epic close to the show features a dancer 'flying' across a huge moon. It's a real spectacle and (conveniently) gives Dion time to change costumes again. Of course, whether she likes it or not, she had to close with this, her biggest hit. Remember what Irving Berlin said about not hating a song that's sold half a million copies - or in this case 15 million.
The grand, theatrical-style bows with the full cast, remind us this is more than just a pop concert, it's a theatrical event. Dion steps down to the house and embraces a woman (maybe a family member), giving her a rose. It's a nice human touch, but don't be fooled, nothing in a show like this is a last minute thought. It's planned, staged and set up for a specific reason, in this case to make Celine Dion look 'real' and sincere to the audience. With all this epic drama going on around her she still has time to reach down and give a rose to a special person in the audience! As she leaves the stage cinematic style credits roll on the screen, again suggesting we have just witnessed something more than a regular concert.

Amy Winehouse - Live At Glastonbury

Winehouse was not in great shape for this concert. It famously closed with her staggering around the audience and punching someone, which isn't something I'd normally recommend. I wanted to analyse an Amy Winehouse concert to see what similarities I might find to more traditional cabaret acts like those you'll find on a cruise ship. Though her show appears loosely structured, as you'll see, she is still following the tried and tested rules of audience participation, emotional triggers and the closing build. Because of her history with drugs and reputation for cutting sets short, there was an electricity in the audience and an air of unpredictability. Everyone was on the edge of their seats, willing her to deliver a great performance.

Opening Section
1. Uptempo hit: 'Tears Dry On Their Own'

A strong, lively hit to open the show.

2. Chat
We instantly see Amy Winehouse as very real. Everyone instantly warms to her because there is no pretence, no 'packaging'. She makes a quick joke about her dress and gets her guitar.

3. Medium: 'Cupid'

4. Chat
Her life was daily fodder for the press so she can afford to be very familiar with the audience right at the start of the show, because they already know her intimately. There is nice

interaction with the audience as she tell us her husband is released from jail in two weeks.

5. Big hit: 'Back To Black'
A big crowd pleaser before she moves into a slow section of ballads.

Love Section
6. Chat
This is a very personal link about how the next song was written. Amy shows herself to be revealing and funny.

7. Slow: 'Wake Up Alone'

8. Slow: 'Some Unholy War'

9. Slow: 'Love Is A Loosing Game'

Middle Section
This is the usual tricky middle section. Like the other singers we've looked at, this section is a slightly random collection of songs - all good, but without an obvious connecting thread.

10. Up: 'Hey Little Rich Girl'
Big change to break the mood after three ballads.

11. Up: 'Message To You Rudy'
After a short funny link she keeps the mood up.

12. Chat
Here Amy credits the band and jokes around. She seems spontaneous, natural and funny. It's endearing because - like everything else in her show - it all very sincere and feels real.

However you approach your chat, that's how it needs to feel to the audience.

13. Up: 'You're Wondering Now'
Towards the end of the song Amy gets the audience clapping along. Everyone likes to clap along to a good song, it's not just for old people and war time sing-alongs. As we covered earlier in the book, it's always best to start the clapping towards the end of the song so the energy is strong when the song has finished.

The Build Section
As with every show we have looked at, we build to the finale with a bang, Bang, BANG! Instead of three songs Amy does a ten minute band section with the band and one big hit. The effect is exactly the same.

14. Up: 'You Know I'm No Good'
Over the vamp Amy gets the audience shouting back at her. It's great audience participation. She then introduces every band member for a solo. At over ten minutes long, this section replaces at least two regular songs. It ends with a great build as one of her backing singers gets the audience to sing-along. It's probably the most energetic piece so far and the perfect way to build towards the finale. Amy eventually gets off the stage and walks up to the audience.

Finale Section (in the house)
15. Up: 'Me and Mr. Jones'
As she sings, a security man lifts Amy into the 'house' (in this case a muddy field). It's dark and a follow spot tracks her as she poses for pictures, shakes hands, almost falls over and yes, punches someone. The audience love her for it. It's about as raw as any performance could be. What she lacks in vocal control (or

any kind of control) she makes up for by just being real.

16. Up: 'Rehab'

You can see how we have gone from the bang, Bang, BANG! build, into the finale with 'Me and Mr Jones' and now her biggest hit 'Rehab'. It's a great ending. As she staggers around singing about trying to get off drugs, the irony can't be lost on anyone. People came to see a genuine rock star and they got one.

Acknowledgements

I'm constantly mindful of how lucky I am to make my living through music. I love my job and it's no surprise how often I get asked for help by other singers who want to do the same thing.

I've always been happy to share whatever I know with other singers and eventually decided to write a few things down to post on my website. What I intended to be a few paragraphs turned into something pretty substantial. As word spread, other pros wanted to get involved and Cabaret Secrets was born.

Thank you to Tom Mitchelson for teaching me how to write; my proof readers Ariel Tal, Stacey Young and Mark Norris; Ben Hickman for his cover design, Philip Dean for his love and support, and everyone who took time out to record interviews with me.

I especially want to thank the following remarkable professionals for permission to reproduce selections from their copyrighted works and for generously sharing their own cabaret secrets with me, so that I could share them with you:

Anthony Davis, Annemarie Lewis Thomas, Barbara Brussell, Barbara Dickson, Barry Robinson, Bettine Clemen, Ben Walters, Carlos Castillo, Chris Peters, Danny Kon, David Ackert, Dean Rudd, Don Black, Eleanor Keenan, Gary England, Gary Parkes, Harry The Piano, Hector Coris, Iain Mackenzie, Jackie Herd, Jan Abrams, Jeannie Deva, Jeff Harnar, Jo Martin, John Martin, Joan Jaffe, Jodi Picoult, Joel Pierson, Joey Mix, John Wilson, Kay

Richardson, Keith Maynard, Kim Gavin, Kuba Kawnik, Lennie Watts, Lisa Cottrell, Lisa Martland, Liz Callaway, Mark Eynon, Mark Norris, Mark Shenton, Marlena Shaw, Marta Sanders, Michael Dore, Michael Feinstein, Neile Adams, Paul Fawcus, Paul L. Martin, Phil Barley, Ruth Leon, Sarah Maxwell, Sinéad Blanchfield, Steven Applegate, Sue Raney, Tara Khaler, Tim Fulker, Tom Derycke and Veronica Ferriani

About The Author

"...the UK's leading standard bearer for the supercool era" is how the London Evening Standard described Gary Williams, star of the West End's 'Rat Pack' and soloist with leading big bands and concert orchestras throughout the world, including the Royal Liverpool Philharmonic, the Melbourne Symphony, the BBC Big Band, the Ulster Orchestra and the Lahti Sinfonia of Finland.

Born in Grimsby, England in 1970, Gary found his voice in community theatre and social clubs before getting his first break with the BBC Big Band. The concert was broadcast on regional radio and caught the attention of BBC bosses, who immediately invited Gary to perform in a series of concerts with the band for Radio 2's Big Band Special and on national television paying tribute to Vic Damone. It was there he met broadcaster David Jacobs who suggested they tour the UK together with a new show 'The Legend of Sinatra', which ran for 12 months prompting the London Times to say, "Michael Bublé isn't the only person keeping the Sinatra flame alive".

After guest appearances with the Syd Lawrence Orchestra, Gary was introduced to conductor and arranger John Wilson leading to numerous concerts with the Northern Sinfonia, City of Birmingham Symphony, Royal Scottish National, RTE Concert Orchestra, Icelandic Sinfonia, Northern Sinfonia and an Australian tour with the Melbourne Symphony and the Adelaide Symphony Orchestras. Their concerts included tributes to Frank Sinatra, Nat 'King' Cole and the MGM Musicals.

Gary has been a regular guest of the BBC Concert Orchestra for 'Friday Night Is Music Night' and had the honour of performing for The Prince of Wales at Buckingham Palace. He starred in the 50th anniversary concert of 'Songs for Swingin' Lovers' with Ireland's RTE Orchestra, presented by Nelson Riddle's daughter Rosemary and subsequently 'Putting on My Top Hat' with Fred Astaire's daughter, Ava. He was invited by the LA Jazz Institute to perform at Frank Sinatra's famous Palm Springs home and for Sinatra's centenary year he presented 'Happy Birthday Mr Sinatra' with the Royal Liverpool Philharmonic and Hallé Orchestras.

In 2004 Gary enjoyed his West End debut, recreating the role of Frank Sinatra for 150 performances of 'The Rat Pack Live From Las Vegas' at The Theatre Royal Haymarket, The Strand and the subsequent European tour to Austria, Switzerland, Denmark, Germany and The Netherlands.

Other work includes a concert The Legend of Sinatra (UK tour), the Nelson Riddle Orchestra in Los Angeles, BBC Pebble Mill, 'That's Entertainment' a tribute to the MGM musicals with the John Wilson Orchestra at the Royal Festival Hall, the 'White Christmas' national orchestral tour including two sell-out concerts at the Royal Albert Hall, Gloria Hunniford's 'Open House' (with Donny Osmond and Burt Bacharach), and the soundtrack for the Warner Bros' motion picture 'Mrs Ratcliffe's Revolution'. Gary performed two new songs for 'Doctor Who – A Celebration' from Cardiff's Millennium Centre complete with Daleks, Cybermen, and the Welsh National Concert Orchestra (broadcast on BBC's Christmas day special and available on BBC DVD). He has appeared on Radio 2's 'Jazz Notes', he's sung live in session for Jazz FM, 'Weekend Wogan' with Richard Madeley, Radio 4's Loose Ends and many times for Gaby Roslin at BBC Radio London.

As a broadcaster he hosts he In Conversation Radio Podcast

and has contributed on Radio 4's consumer programme 'You and Yours'. He wrote and presented a two-hour tribute to show called 'Sinatra, My Hero' for BBC Radio Humberside, broadcast on Christmas day.

Gary is one of the UK's most respected cabaret performers and a fixture at London's Ronnie Scott's, the Pheasantry and the Crazy Coqs. His shows include Sinatra Jukebox (Bestival), Let There Be Love (celebrating Nat 'King' Cole), Hollywood Swings and That's Life. His annual seasonal show 'A Swingin' Christmas' was given four stars by The Times and five stars by the London Evening Standard who called it, "The jolliest sleigh ride in town".

He's literally written the book on stagecraft 'Cabaret Secrets: How to create your own show, travel the world and get paid to do what you love', described by The Times as, "a fascinating insider's handbook".

Internationally Gary has presented concerts in Florence, Australia, Portugal, Finland, Iceland, Oslo, Jordan (for the British Council) and Japan including Birdland Tokyo.

A regular headliner for the world's largest cruise lines, Gary has visited over 60 countries including such varied places as Alaska, Brazil (for two seasons with his Latin show), the Falkland Islands, Hawaii, China and Libya. As a presenter he's recorded corporate films for numerous clients including Sainsbury's, McCain, the Health Protection Authority, Seafish and Jessops Cameras.

Gary has entertained numerous private and corporate audiences at The Ritz, The Savoy, The Dorchester, The Playboy Club, Soho House, The Ivy, Mossiman's, The Pigalle, The Houses of Parliament, Alexander Palace and Spencer House. For two years Gary and his musicians were resident at the Royal Garden Hotel's 'Manhattan Nights'.

Gary is the recipient the Outstanding Support Award from

children's charity When You Wish Upon A Star and was recently given the RNLI's Bronze Award. In recognition of his work for the Caron Keating Foundation he was invited by the Prime Minister to Downing Street.

He has recorded three solo albums at Abbey Road Studios, projects for the Reader's Digest 'Timeless Classics' series, with the Royal Ballet Sinfonia for 'What A Carry On', and with the Syd Lawrence Orchestra for Sinatra tribute album which was Jazz FM's album of the week. His live Nat Cole tribute album with the Ronnie Scott's house band, prompted Oscar winning lyricist Don Black to say, "In a world of Pop Idol mediocrity Gary Williams shines like a dazzling beacon." Treasure Seeker, his first album as singer/songwriter counts Leslie Bricusse, another Oscar winner, among its fans. He said, "There is a dreamy, easy-going timelessness about the songs, shades of Rodgers and Hart one minute, Antonio Carlos Jobim the next. Songs like these make you want the ghosts of Mel Tormé and Matt Monro to come back and sing them. Until they do, Gary Williams is their worthy guardian."

For more advice, free Podcasts and one-to-one Cabaret Masterclasses, visit: cabaretsecrets.com

Index

A

Abbey Road 104
Abrams, Jan 30
Ackert, David 191
Adams, Neile 24
ad-libbing 53, 61-62
advice (giving it and getting it) 108-111
agents (and how to get one) 154-166,
anecdotes 56-58, 181, 212
Applegate, Steven 22, 30
arrangements (musical) 71-83, 162
Astaire, Fred 51
audience participation 67-70

B

Barley, Phil 130
Baylis, Trevor 185
Bennett, Tony 85, 173, 179
Berlin, Irving 43, 112, 221
Blair, Robert 183
Blanchfield, Sinead 102, 104
Boyzone 12
Brussell, Barbara 32, 34, 38, 63, 118
Bublé, Michael 185-186, 214-217
Buckingham Palace 6

C

Callaway, Ann Hampton 31, 182
Callaway, Liz 19, 21, 31, 32, 63, 183
Castillo, Carlos 135
chat. *See* patter

Chenoweth, Kristen 30
Clemen, Bettine 80
Cole, Nat 'King' 58, 76
comedy 26, 54–62, 87, 115, 161, 174. *See also* jokes
confidence 13, 176, 191
Cook, Barbara 2, 182
Coris, Hector 123, 128, 159
Cottrell, Lisa 9, 14, 23, 49, 51
Cowell, Simon 11, 173–179
criticism. *See* advice (giving it and getting it)
cruise ships 4, 45, 48, 51, 59, 75, 85, 94, 111, 115, 122, 159, 171, 174

D

Damone, Vic 110
Davis Jr., Sammy 52
Davis, Anthony 14
Derycke, Tom 85
Deva, Jeannie 141–149
Dickson, Barbara 182, 183
Dietrich, Marlene 96
Digifiles (and Digipaks) 105
Dion, Céline 2, 45, 212, 218
director (hiring a) 48, 118, 121
Don't Tell Mama 28
Dore, Michael 57, 140, 151
Dylan, Bob 187

E

England, Gary 30
EPK (Electronic Press Kit) 157

F

Facebook 125, 129-134
Farah, Mo 51
Fawcus, Paul 90, 92, 93, 102-107
fear 5, 14, 51, 171, 192
Feinstein, Michael 56, 65, 88, 108, 182, 189
Ferriani, Veronica 41, 63
focus 64
foreign languages 113
Foster, David 186

fourth wall (the) 1, 4, 27, 29, 67, 198, 210, 216
Friedman, Maria 30
Fulker, Tim 71

G

Garland, Judy 86, 108, 118
Gavin, Kim 11, 35, 52, 119, 190
Gershwin 56
gimmicks 160
Google Alerts 127
graphic designers 104

H

Harnar, Jeff 19, 48, 87, 119, 174, 189
Harry the Piano 133
Herd, Jackie 105-106
Hill, Benny 55
Hristov, Vasil 95, 114

I

IMAG 95, 200
instrumental breaks 75
ISRC codes 105, 200

J

Jackson, Michael 52, 173
Jaffe, Joan 13
jokes 21, 58–60, 69, 109, 210-212, 215, 219, 223. *See also* comedy
Jungr, Barb 182

K

Kawnik, Kuba 93, 110
Keenan, Eleanor 49, 64, 72, 152, 182
Khaler, Tara 2, 33, 50, 77, 112, 176
King, Maria 161, 176
Kon, Danny 95

L

length of show 46

Leob, Lisa 187
Leon, Ruth 155, 165
Lewis, Leona 12
lighting 84–101
lighting directions 85
López, Sharon 161
lost luggage 167
Luft, Lorna 117

M

Mackenzie, Iain 14, 57, 149
make-up 98
Marcovicci, Andrea 1, 4, 191
marketing your show 122-137
Martin, John 59
Martin, Jo 135, 159, 163
Martin, Paul L. 3, 62, 190
Martland, Lisa 2, 4, 128, 130, 180
Maxwell, Sarah 99
Maynard, Keith 112, 164, 175, 178
Messi, Leo 51
microphone technique 91
Minnelli, Liza 2, 125
missing the ship 171
Mix, Joey 22, 77–78
Monro, Matt 209
Mozart 111
musicians (working with) 15, 71–83

N

networking 125
Norris, Mark 117, 118
notes. *See* advice (giving it and getting it)

O

open mics 125, 189
Osmond, Donny 119

P

Pareto's principle 121

Parkes, Gary 112, 157, 178
patter 29, 46–64, 78, 110, 111
Peters, Chris 88
Picoult, Jodi 23
Pierson, Joel 70, 75
print media 122
production (adding elements of) 89
publicist 117–119, 132

R

Rácz, Máté 161
Raney, Sue 181
recording a CD 98–102, 192
Reeves, Martha 158
rehearsing 76
rejection 178
Richardson, Kay 87, 89
rider 87
riser 90, 195
Rivers, Joan 156
Robinson, Barry 51, 69, 70, 111, 167
Ross, Steve 52, 71, 82, 172
Royal Albert Hall 81
Rudd, Dean 94
Ruiz, Hector 115
rule of threes 58

S

Sanders, Marta 13, 24, 53, 55, 60, 103
scrim 90, 195
Shaw, Marlena 49
Shenton, Mark 3, 11, 47, 98, 122, 124, 173
Short, Bobby 12
showreel 152
Sinatra, Frank 2, 52, 145, 178, 182, 211
sincerity 11, 13, 29, 30, 48, 55, 63
social media 124
sore throat 144
sound 86
specialising 176
Stage Newspaper 24, 107

stage clothes 91
Stealing 62
Stritch, Elaine 3, 30, 48

T

Take That 2, 12, 35, 52
template 32–47, 209
theme 1, 19-21, 33–35, 65
Thomas, Annemarie Lewis 29, 50
Thomas, Clive 61, 156, 183
travel advice 167
Twitter 128-137

V

vocal care 138-153
vocal cool down 147
vocal warm up 140-149

W

Walters, Ben 25, 61, 67, 122, 127
Watts, Lennie 12, 28, 66, 119
websites 134–136
West, Sam 140, 149
Whiting, Margaret 182
Wilson, John 13, 15, 184
Winehouse, Amy 222
Wolf, João 20, 49, 114, 116, 171, 177
Working Men's Clubs 9, 112

X

The 'X' factor 11–15, 173, 190

Y

YouTube 121, 133-134, 136, 157